GT
732
.C84
1969

Cunnington, Cecil
Willett

Handbook of Eng-
lish mediaeval
costume

DATE DUE

JUL 19 '78	MAY 2 9 2002		
FEB 0			

The Library
Onondaga Community College
Rte. 173, Onondaga Hill
Syracuse, New York 13215

Handbook of
English Mediaeval Costume

A 13TH CENTURY COSTUME

Embroidered tunic with typical 'magyar'
sleeves. Mantle lined with vair fur. Decorative soled hose.

HANDBOOK OF
ENGLISH MEDIAEVAL
COSTUME

by

C. WILLETT CUNNINGTON, *1878- 1961*
and
PHILLIS CUNNINGTON

with illustrations by
BARBARA PHILLIPSON
and Catherine Lucas

FABER AND FABER LIMITED
3 Queen Square
London

First published in 1952
by Faber and Faber Limited
3 Queen Square London W.C.1
Reprinted (with corrections) 1960
Second edition 1969
Second edition reprinted with corrections 1973
Printed in Great Britain
by John Dickens & Co Ltd Northampton
All rights reserved

ISBN 0 571 04670 3

Contents

Preface to the First Edition

The aim of this Handbook is to present in a concise form a systematic account of English Mediaeval Costume, from A.D. 800 to A.D. 1500.

The material has been obtained from illustrations in illuminated MSS., church effigies, brasses, and from contemporary literature. We have availed ourselves of the extensive researches by those authors mentioned in the bibliography, and to whom we are much indebted. We also wish to thank the Essex Archaeological Society, whose invaluable library at Colchester has been of very great help, the Essex Record Office, Chelmsford, and the authorities in charge of the British Museum Library, the Victoria and Albert Museum Library, The John Rylands Library, Manchester, the Fitzwilliam Museum, Cambridge, the Trinity College Library, Cambridge, Colchester Castle Museum, Peterborough Museum, Durham Cathedral Library, Exeter Cathedral Library, Hereford Cathedral Library, and Ripon Cathedral Library.

Care has been taken to check all dates from contemporary sources; and those given indicate the limits of a 'fashion', though doubtless exceptions occur outside these limits. The line drawings, made under our supervision, serve to clarify verbal descriptions. Some foreign sources have been preferred to English ones where they provided clearer illustrations of identical fashions. Thus a 'butterfly headdress' is better understood in a foreign picture than in an English brass. The coloured illustrations are intended to represent the types of colour schemes employed, and do not profess to be replicas of originals.

The nomenclature used by mediaeval writers was confusing, often with names applied to more than one garment, or with several names for one and the same thing. We have simplified this, and relegated to a glossary terms of uncertain or irregular use. In the description of the various garments we have included only those forms for which there is reliable evidence that they were in use in this country, and no positive fact has been stated which has not been confirmed from authentic sources.

As a reference book the arrangement of the material has been designed to facilitate accurate and ready dating of mediaeval illustrations, effigies, brasses, etc. It may also serve as a companion to the larger works on the subject and as a convenient guide to the stage costumier. For Underclothes see our 'History of Underclothes', 1951.

Foreign evidence is valuable provided that we allow for the 'time-lag' which elapsed, especially from the fourteenth century onwards, before such fashions were adopted here; and that we eliminate those which seem never to have crossed the Channel.

A single fragment of evidence must be accepted with caution. Thus in *Eulogium Historiarum* [c. 1420] is the statement so much copied by later writers, that the long toes of piked shoes (tempus Richard II) were even supported by chains to the knee.* Fairholt, in his *Costume in England*, 1860, specifically stated that this fashion 'is well authenticated by contemporary narrators', but gave no references; and subsequent writers have entirely failed to discover any. It has been suggested that perhaps it was a mode displayed by the courtiers coming here with Anne of Bohemia. There seems no evidence that it became an *English* fashion, and we follow Mr Kelly in ignoring it.

Knitting was in use in the reign of Queen **Mary.**[1] Yet we find in the Household Accounts of Sir John Fastolf [c. 1450] mention of a 'knitted cap', and M. Harmand says he has found similar references in the fifteenth century. We do not know whether such

---

[1] (1557). 'Item pd for the knytting of ii paire of hosen for Mr. George Farmer 14d.' Essex Record Office (D.DP. A9c.)

Footnote to Second edition. Actually the statement does not occur in the *Eulogium* (late 14th c. with additions up to c. 1420). It was given, without mention of source, by John Stow in the 1604 edition of his *Summerie of the Chronicles of England*, though not in the first edition (1565). Joseph Camden, in the 1614 edition of his *Remaines*, definitely attributes the same statement to the *Eulogium*. Its true origin remains obscure.

isolated examples were 'foreign imports', but they cannot justifiably be described as a 'fashion'. We reserve that term for styles proved by contemporary evidence to have been in general use; while those which were less common—though not unique— we call 'rare'.

Preface to the Second Edition

For the second edition of the Handbook new sections on the dress of working people and on children's costume have been added, incorporating the results of recent research on these lesser known subjects.

The entire Handbook has been revised. As regards the illustrations, many new figures have been introduced, and a number of improvements made, in some places by substituting English for foreign examples, and in others by using direct instead of indirect sources. Care has been taken to give detailed references for the sources of all the figures. The bibliography has been brought up to date and there is a new index.

I am greatly indebted to Miss Catherine Lucas M.Sc., for writing the section on the dress of working people and for the large amount of work she has carried out in revising the text and illustrations.

Phillis Cunnington
York, 1968.

Ninth and Tenth Centuries

MEN

1. THE TUNIC

A loose garment worn next to the shirt and put on over the head.

Length

(*a*) Short, about knee-length, and sometimes slit up at the sides.

(*b*) Long, ankle length, usually worn by nobility on ceremonial occasions.

Neck

(*a*) Round, with enough room for the head to pass.

(*b*) Round, with a short vertical slit in front.

(*c*) Square.

Sleeves

(*a*) Close fitting to wrist, usually with many circular puckers round forearm giving plenty of play. The sleeves were probably made to reach beyond the hand.

(*b*) Sometimes loose and open (with long tunics).

Girdles. Narrow sashes, almost invariably worn.

Embroidery. At neck, wrists, hem and girdle, in coloured silks, was common. Precious stones added for ceremonial garments.

Materials. Linen for the wealthy, wool for the poorer.

2. THE SUPER-TUNIC OR OUTER TUNIC

'ROC' was the Saxon name (hence the word 'frock'). Worn over the tunic, was loose fitting and put on over the head through a wide neck opening.

9

1. 10TH CENTURY

(a) Long, square-necked tunic, over which is worn a draped mantle. 'Phrygian bonnet'. (b) Short tunic with close puckered sleeves. Cloak clasped on right shoulder. Loose stockings. Shoes. (c) Metal fillet. Embroidered neck of tunic. (d) Short tunic with girdle. Alternative neck line. (a) and (d) *c.* 1000 A.D. (b) and (c) 971-984.

Length

(*a*) Long, but revealing the bottom of the tunic. The long super-tunic was worn over the long ceremonial tunic by persons of rank, and was usually embroidered round the neck, sleeves and hem. Sometimes made of silk. Its sleeves were full and open to elbow or wrist; or, rarely, tight-fitting.

(*b*) Short. Sleeves tight-fitting to wrist, or, very rarely, loose.

Girdles. Optional with both forms.

3. THE CLOAK OR MANTLE

Cut on the square and not on a circle. Varied from a short cape to a long flowing mantle, the latter chiefly reserved for the nobility.

Worn over tunic or super-tunic.

Fastenings

(*a*) By brooch or clasp on right shoulder, leaving right arm free. Vice versa for left-handed men.

(*b*) By ties, brooch or clasp in front.

No Hoods (as in the twelfth century)

In the tenth century, the mantle in the shape of a large oblong shawl was sometimes worn wrapped round the body from the waist, forming a loose shapeless skirt, the free end being draped over the left or right shoulder.

4. THE CLOSED MANTLE

Large and square, with a hole in the centre for slipping over the head. Worn without brooch or buckle. For men and women of the highest rank only.

Mantles of all kinds (particularly those for women) were often lined with material of a different colour, e.g. red lined with blue. Lined mantles are here referred to as "double mantles".

5. THE BRATT

A short coarse wrap or cloak worn by peasants (not to be confused with the dialect 'brat' for apron).

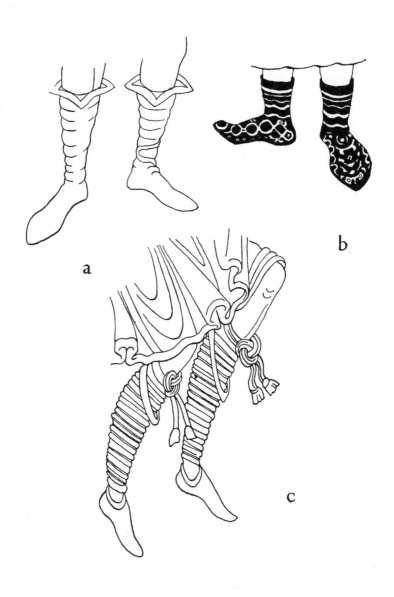

a

b

c

2. 9TH AND 10TH CENTURIES

(a) Long boots (9th c.). (b) Short boots, decorated (9th c.). (c) Leg bandages and shoes (971-984).

6. LEGWEAR

(1) BRAIES OR DRAWERS were moderately loose-fitting breeches, tied on just below the waist by a running string, and ending above or below the knee. If below they were somewhat close-fitting and secured by ties. Worn by all classes.

(2) LONG BRAIES, like trousers, reached to the ankles and were sometimes slit at the base. Often bound from knee to ankle with bandages. Worn by all classes.

(3) HOSE, corresponding to stockings, a word not used in this limited sense until the late sixteenth century. To avoid confusion, however, the term 'stockings' will be used instead of 'hose' wherever stockings in the modern sense are meant.

Either long to thighs, usually worn by the rich, often made of linen. Or short, barely reaching the knees, and when of wool worn by the rustics and poorer classes.

Both kinds were often brightly coloured.

(4) SOCKS. Worn with long braies or with over stockings; also often brightly coloured and having decorative borders.

(5) LEG BANDAGES were strips of linen or wool bound spirally over stockings or trousers from foot or ankle to just below the knee. The criss-cross arrangement was confined to royalty and high ecclesiastics. Their bandages were often embroidered.

Leg bandages might replace stockings, being worn like puttees with the ends tucked in at the top, or tied and left dangling if tasselled.

7. FOOTWEAR

(1) SHOES shaped to the foot, distinguishing right from left, and slightly pointed opposite the big toe. The raised heel was unknown throughout the Middle Ages.

Styles

(a) Fairly wide opening round ankle.

(b) Close round ankle, with central slit down the top of the foot.

(c) Close round ankle with side slits leaving a centre flap.

Fastenings

(a) By thongs attached behind, passed round the ankle and tied over instep in front.

(*b*) No fastenings.

Materials. Chiefly leather. Soles of leather or wood, and sometimes reinforced by studding with nails.

(2) BOOTS, reaching to mid-calf, or shorter. Loose or tied with thongs. Often decorated.

(3) WOODEN CLOGS sometimes worn.

(4) SLIPPERS, with open tops and low vamps, worn by the clergy and women.

8. HEADWEAR

(1) NONE. It was the fashion to go bareheaded.

(2) PLAIN METAL FILLETS.

(3) THE 'PHRYGIAN BONNET'. A small cap with a pointed crown curved forwards. A number of slight variations in shape and decoration occurred.

Worn until the beginning of the thirteenth century. *Materials.* Skins of animals, wool and felt.

9. HAIR

Young men wore thick hair waving back from the forehead and temples, sometimes with a short centre parting, to nape of neck or lower. Clean shaven face. Older men wore their hair waving down from a centre parting or a fringe, to neck or shoulders. Whiskers, moustaches, and long beards often forked and pointed, were usual.

10. ACCESSORIES

Wallets, slung from the shoulders or girdle.

Bracelets, generally of gold, and rings of gold or metal.

Shoulder Belts, passing over the right shoulder to left side, from which was slung a sword. (Nobility only.)

Gloves (imported from the Continent), worn only by the nobility and clergy of high rank.

11. COLOURS

Red, blue, green, pink, violet, purple and yellow. Gold and silver thread much used in embroidery.

An example of Saxon embroidery is the stole and maniple made for Bishop Fridestan, found in St. Cuthbert's coffin, and now in Durham Cathedral library.

Ninth and Tenth Centuries

WOMEN

1. THE TUNIC, or KIRTLE (see Glossary)

Worn over the smock (i.e. chemise), and put on over the head. Ground length, the hem sometimes embroidered. Sleeves long and close.

Materials. Linen for the wealthy.
                Wool, often coarsely woven, for the poor.

2. THE SUPER-TUNIC, or ROC

Worn over the tunic by women of all classes, and put on over the head. A loose garment, ground length but frequently hitched up over the girdle exposing the tunic often up to knee level.

Generally lined with material of different colour (in tenth century).

Round neck usually hidden by veil draperies.

Sleeves

(1) Loose and cylindrical.

(2) Loose, broadening from shoulder to a wide bell-shaped opening below the elbow (tenth century).

Embroidered borders at neck, hem, sleeves, and very rarely a strip down the front.

Girdle. A wide sash, always the same colour as the gown, was essential.

3. THE MANTLE

Cut on the square, three-quarter to full length of the tunic, though usually hitched up in front. Fastened under the chin, probably by brooch or tie, the closure being hidden under the

3. 10TH CENTURY

(a) Super-tunic sleeve, with puckered and embroidered tunic sleeve
emerging. Long veil. (b) Tunic with embroidered hem. Embroidered
mantle. Long veil. Shoes. (Both 971–984).

drapery of the veil. Sometimes worn as a shawl, and usually lined with a contrasting colour (tenth century).

The CLOSED MANTLE, identical with that worn by men.

4. HOSE or STOCKINGS
Presumably worn, but never seen.

5. FOOTWEAR
(1) SHOES, of the same shape as the men's.
    (a) With short centre slit over instep.
    (b) Open over foot, with short tongued upper (rare).
Colours. Usually black. Sometimes red, brown, orange or blue.
(2) CLOGS made of wood were worn.

6. HEADWEAR
THE VEIL OR HEAD-RAIL (synonymous terms) was indispensable; worn by all classes, even in bed, though sometimes discarded in intimate domestic life.

A queen's crown was worn over her veil.

It consisted of a long broad scarf, wide enough to reach from the forehead over the back of the head, so as to drape the shoulders, completely concealing the hair and leaving only the face visible. The long ends, passing over the shoulders, were crossed in front over the bosom and reached as low as the knees. It was draped in various ways, one end usually hanging free, the other tucked into the folds at the neck.

Materials. Fine or coarse, according to social position. Bright colours were common, matching or contrasting with the supertunic.

7. HAIR
Though concealed, there are on record 'golden hair ties and crispin needles to curl and plait the hair withal'.

8. ACCESSORIES
Jewellery
Head bands, circlets of gold, diadems and gold neckbands.

Rings, bracelets, ear-rings, beads and jewelled girdles are re-corded though not depicted.

Examples (from Anglo-Saxon wills of the first half of the tenth century). 'Her best dun tunic . . . the better of her cloaks . . . her black tunics . . . her best holy veil . . . her best head band. . . .'

Note. Linen was expensive and used only by the rich (of both sexes).

Wool used by all.

Haircloth chiefly worn by the clergy.

Embroidery, known as 'English work', was celebrated through-out the Continent.

Eleventh Century

MEN

1. THE TUNIC

Fitting slightly closer to the body than the Saxon tunic, but widening to a full skirt. Put on over the head, with a low round neck or with a short slit down the front and fastened with a brooch.

Length
    (*a*) Short, knee or calf length. Worn by all classes.
    (*b*) Long, ankle length. Chiefly worn by higher ranks on ceremonial occasions.

Sleeves. Moderately loose above, but narrowing to a good fit at the wrist.

Girdles, usual but often hidden. The short tunic was further shortened by being drawn up through the girdle so as to overhang it, or being hitched up by the braies girdle underneath.

The skirt of the short tunic sometimes slit up at the sides.

Decoration. Broad embroidered bands, woven or of appliqué work, round the neck, hem and wrists, and sometimes round the upper arm.

Materials with simple all-over designs were also used.

2. THE SUPER-TUNIC[1]

Worn over the tunic. A loose garment put on over the head and made on a circular pattern.

Length. Either the same as that of the tunic or a little shorter, the lower border of the tunic being thus visible.

Sleeves. Loose, often expanding towards the wrists where they were sometimes turned back into a broad cuff. Also close fitting.

[1] Descriptive term used here for men's and women's over-garment.

4. 11TH CENTURY

(a) Belted short tunic with embroidery on skirt, shoulder and cuff. Embroidered cloak, knotted on shoulder. Criss-cross leg bandages. Shoes. No supertunic. (*c.* 1050). (b) Supertunic short with unusually narrow sleeves, short tunic showing below. Cloak clasped. Leg bandages. (c) Old man in long cloak. Tunic, contrasting border, side vents. Forked beard. (d) Old man in long supertunic and tunic. Bare feet.

Girdles. Optional, and used, as for the tunic, to hitch up and shorten the garment.

3. THE CLOAK

A loose wrap, rectangular or semicircular in cut; varied in length from knee to ankle. Fastened by tie or brooch, under the chin or on the shoulder. Dignitaries and the elderly still wore it draped as before.

Mantles of the nobility were of finer materials, often lined with fur, and usually long. Fastened by a cord threaded through attached metal rings sewn to opposite edges, a method only used by persons of rank.

Hooded cloaks were introduced at the end of the century, worn chiefly by travellers or rustics, and made of wool or skins.

4. LEGWEAR

(1) BRAIES OR "BREECHES" were loose drawers, sometimes reaching to the ankle and fastened above by a threaded cord 'en coulisse' and tied well below waist level. The cord was sometimes made of leather, and usually emerged at intervals, the exposed portions serving in the twelfth century as points of attachment for long stockings, wallets, etc.

The legs of the breeches were:

(a) Fitted to the leg from knee to ankle, a style for the nobility.

(b) Loose fitting to the ankle and sometimes slit up behind for a variable distance; the type worn by the common people.

Both styles, but chiefly the loose variety, were made to fit the leg more closely by means of stockings drawn on over the breeches up to the knee, or by means of leg bandages.

(2) LEG BANDAGES were strips of linen or wool, bound spirally (or by the higher ranks in a criss-cross pattern) from foot or ankle to below the knee over the trouser leg or stockings. Ceased to be fashionable after 1100, though worn later occasionally by rustics, but reappeared in the thirteenth century for a short period as a fashion for the nobility and then bound criss-cross and reaching above the knees.

(3) STOCKINGS (hose or chausses) were of wool or linen, cut

5. 11TH CENTURY

(a) Norman hair-style (late 11th c.) (b) Young man displays a super-tunic (with broad ornamented border) holding it by the sleeves. (c) Conical cap. (d) Stockings with ornamental tops, oversocks, shoes, bordered tunic (c. 1050). (e) Similar, without oversock. (f) Closed mantle, 'Phrygian' cap, money-bag.

to the shape of the leg. (Knitting, as a craft, was unknown in England until the second half of the sixteenth century.) They reached to just below the knee, very rarely above, often ending with an ornamental border which may have served as a garter. Sometimes instead of having a foot the stocking ended in a stirrup.

5. FOOTWEAR

(1) SHOES were pointed and shaped to the foot, distinguishing right from left. No raised heels. Usually of leather, with decorative patterns on the shoes of the nobility.

Forms

(*a*) Closed to the ankle with a short tongue over the instep.

(*b*) Slit down over the instep and fastened with an ankle thong.

(2) BOOTS. Short and fastened with thongs, were uncommon in the eleventh century.

6. HEADWEAR

(1) BARE-HEADED, which was fashionable through the eleventh, twelfth and thirteenth centuries.

(2) THE HOOD attached to the cloak.

(3) THE SAXON 'PHRYGIAN CAP', with a liking for the straight pointed variety.

7. HAIR

Up to 1087.

The older men wore their hair medium long to nape of neck, with centre parting or shaggy fringe. Beards often forked and moustaches of medium length. Moustache alone extremely rare, but beards without moustaches quite common, the face being clean shaven round the mouth. The younger men were clean-shaven. Their hair was brushed back from the forehead with or without a centre parting, and fell to the neck or shoulders. Some Norman youths had short hair which was shaved at the back of the head. This was a limited fashion supposed to originate from Aquitaine.

Later. 1087 to 1150, but moderated from 1100 to 1125, all men, young and old, allowed their hair and beards to grow as long as possible, some curling, crimping and plaiting them.

8. ACCESSORIES

The *Girdle* was a plain band or cord.

Gloves were almost unknown.

Aprons were worn by the lower classes.

Swords were not worn by civilians throughout the Middle Ages, being a badge of knighthood.

The *purse* or *pouch* was a money-bag tied round its neck (Fig. 5f).

Eleventh Century

WOMEN

1. THE GOWN or KIRTLE

Corresponding to the masculine Tunic, but always long, more or less ground length. Worn over the smock (chemise), it was loose, cut like the male tunic, and always worn with a girdle.

Sleeves. Close fitting, and tight at the wrist.

2. THE SUPER-TUNIC or ROC

A long loose garment worn over the Kirtle, probably for warmth; similar in design to the male super-tunic.

Sleeves. Loose, expanding to a wide opening at the wrist, though occasionally moderately close fitting.

Some were tubular and extended well beyond the hand acting as a muff.

3. THE CLOAK or MANTLE

Similar to the male garment, but almost invariably of ground length and generally closed, i.e. put on over the head. Could be worn over the kirtle without super-tunic.

Cloaks for women were not hooded.

4. LEGWEAR

No braies or drawers were worn by women (in fact, not until the nineteenth century).

Stockings or Hose, of cloth, similar to the men's but sometimes reaching above the knees; kept up by ties.

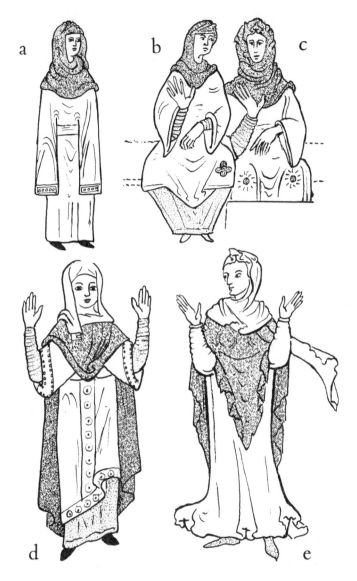

6. 11TH CENTURY

(a) Supertunic sleeves long, to cover the hands. (b) Supertunic embroidered at knee. Kirtle, its tight sleeves and skirt showing. Veil, probably open. (c) Similar. Veil closed. (d) Closed cloak. Supertunic embroidered, hitched up by girdle. Kirtle, its sleeves and skirt showing. Open veil. Shoes. (e) Closed cloak. Kirtle. Scarf-like veil.

5. FOOTWEAR
Shoes similar to those worn by men.

6. HEADWEAR
THE VEIL, Coverchief or Kerchief (French—couvre-chef), corresponding to the Saxon head-rail (from antiquity to the end of the Middle Ages), but smaller, was rectangular or part of a circle. One straight edge hung over the forehead, concealing the hair; the rest falling in draperies round the face and neck, and often crossed over or joined in front, thus encircling the face. Occasionally it was long and wound round like a scarf.

7. HAIR
Flowing loose and uncovered was a mode only allowed for young girls. Otherwise it was concealed.

ACCESSORIES
As for the tenth century.

Twelfth Century

MEN

1. THE TUNIC[1]

As in the eleventh century, but new variations appeared.

(*a*) With close fitting body, and long skirt generally slit up in front to thigh level, and worn with or without a girdle which for the aristocracy might carry a sword.

Sleeves fairly close fitting with a sudden bell-shaped expansion at the wrist, or with the lower portion hanging to form a pendulous cuff which might be rolled up for action. (1130s to 1170s). Compare with the more exaggerated form worn by women. Tight-fitting ornamental turn-back cuffs were an alternative.

(*b*) Short, with loose tubular sleeves often rolled back at the wrist.

Worn by peasants and social inferiors.

(*c*) Cut in a style characteristic of the thirteenth century, with Magyar sleeves, and the front of the skirt cut up to the girdle (End of twelfth century to 1300).

New Neck Line, in which the front slit might be:

(1) Diagonal from neck across the chest, or

(2) Horizontal from neck to shoulder.

These new neck lines appeared in any tunic from the end of the twelfth to early fourteenth centuries, but were uncommon.

2. THE SUPER-TUNIC[2]

Similar to that of the eleventh century. A girdle was optional. Occasionally worn alone, with a girdle, but not worn with tunics of style (*a*).

---

[1] and [2] Descriptive terms retained, since authorities differ regarding the names actually in use.

7. 12TH CENTURY

(a) Fur-lined cloak, jewelled clasp on shoulder. Short-sleeved super-
tunic. Long tunic. Soled hose. Hair style of young man. Hat. (*c.* 1170).
(b) Shepherd in hooded cloak, short tunic with rolled up sleeves.
Short decorated boots. Long forked beard. (*c.* 1155). (c) Tunic with
pendulous cuffs; slit skirt showing long hose, probably soled (p. 31),
drawn up over braies (*c.* 1170). (d) Youth (David). Tunic. Short boots.
(e) Old man (Samuel anointing). Wide-sleeved supertunic over long
tunic. Long closed mantle. Note hair style (*c.* 1155).

29

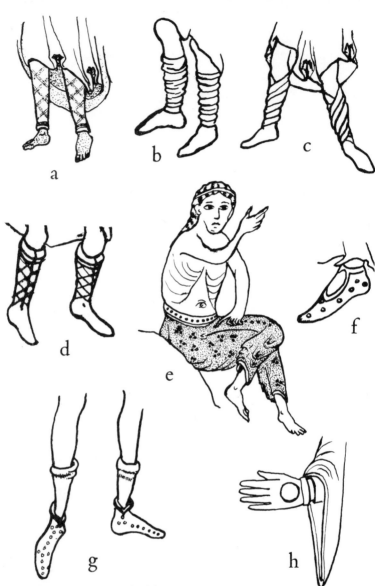

8. 12TH CENTURY

(a) Footless hose, patterned, worn for walking. (b) Short stockings slipping down. Shoes (*c.* 1170). (c) Leg bandages of a shepherd. (d) Long boots. (e) Job (in sickness). Long, coloured, embroidered braies (1108-1124). (f) Strap shoes. (g) Short stockings, high shoes. (h) Jewelled glove (*c.* 1190). [(a), (c), (d) and (f) *c.* 1155].

Sleeves. (*a*) With pendulous cuffs; uncommon.

(*b*) Loose, and often elbow-length only.

Pelisson is a super-tunic lined with fur (Came in *c.* 1165).

3. THE CLOAK and MANTLE

As in the eleventh century. A new variety was a very small cloak lined with fur.

Common method of fastening: The upper corner of the neck edge on one side was pulled through a ring sewn to the opposite corner, and then knotted to keep it in position. Otherwise ornamental clasp or brooch used.

Materials. Mantles for the nobility of rich materials frequently lined with fur.

Cloaks for rustics usually hooded and often made of skins worn with the hairy surface outside.

4. LEGWEAR

(1) BRAIES, similar to those of the eleventh century continued for the first half of the twelfth. They then became shortened to the knee, becoming drawers (i.e. under-garments) in the second half of the century, and were chiefly made of linen.

(2) STOCKINGS

(*a*) Short, ending below knee often with ornamental border.

(*b*) Long, reaching to mid-thigh, and shaped to fit the leg, widening above the knee so that they could be pulled up over the braies. They usually ended in a pointed tongue in front from which a tie attached the stocking to the breech girdle at a point of emergence from the coulisse.

Some hose had stirrups instead of whole feet (Cf. Fig. 22a); others had no feet at all.

Footed hose with a thin leather sole attached (Saxon, then 1160s to end of fifteenth century), were worn without shoes, and were made of stout woollen material or even of thin leather. (King John had a pair of cowhide.)

Colours were bright, and stripes were popular.

The finer qualities were very costly.

9. 12TH CENTURY

(a) Small round cap with stalk. (a) and (b) Tunics (old style). Cloaks. Long stockings and long boots. (1121–48). (c) Coif. Hood thrown back. (Late 12th c.). (d) Tunic with 'magyar' sleeves. 'Phrygian' cap. Long stockings. Short pointed boots. (Late 12th c.). (e) Cloak clasped on left shoulder. (f) Hooded cloak. (g) Large hat. (1121–48.) [(e) and (g) composite drawings].

5. FOOTWEAR

Boots and shoes worn by all classes.

(1) SHOES

(a) Open over the foot and fastened in front of the ankle with a strap secured by brooch or buckle. For the wealthy these shoes had ornamental bands or decorative designs over the foot or round the heel.

(b) High round the ankle and slit down the sides or in front. Sometimes laced up.

(c) Shoes with short uppers but cut high behind the heel began to appear (end of twelfth century).

(2) BOOTS

(a) Reaching to mid calf or knee; laced on the inner side or down the centre; often with brightly coloured turn-over tops.

(b) Short, reaching just above the ankle.

Shaped as in the eleventh century, but often more pointed. (The long-pointed shoes described in contemporary writings as of exaggerated length are not, however, seen in illustrations of the time.)

Materials for footwear: Leather (cowhide or oxhide), cloth, fish-skin, and sometimes silk.

6. HEADWEAR

(1) THE HOOD, as a separate entity [1160 to 1460] was the most characteristic covering; a loose pointed cowl with attached cape reaching the shoulders.

The *cape,* known as the *gorget,* was usually closed all round, so that the hood had to be put on over the head. When open in front (far less usual form) it was fastened at the neck by brooch or clasp.

(2) THE POINTED PHRYGIAN CAP. (Tenth to end of twelfth century, and unfashionably into the thirteenth.)

(3) SMALL ROUND CAP with a stalk; or with a rolled brim and with or without a stalk.

(4) A STALKED SOFT CAP, resembling a beret.

(5) HATS with large brims and low crowns were worn by travellers, and frequently over the hood. Usually there were two

strings which when loosely tied under the chin enabled the hat to be thrown back on to the neck without falling off.

(6) SMALL HAT with round crown and turned-down brim, decorated with a knob instead of a stalk.

(7) THE COIF (end of twelfth century to 1440, after which used by professions). A close fitting plain linen bonnet (resembling a baby's bonnet) which covered the ears and confined the hair; tied under the chin. Worn either alone or under any other type of headgear.

Gold or silver *fillets*, often jewelled, were worn by nobles.

7. HAIR

Long hair to the shoulders and long beards and moustaches were usual. The hair was often parted on either side of the head, the central portion being brought forward in a shaggy fringe over the forehead. These styles were slightly shorter all round, for a few years at the beginning and the end of the twelfth century. (The moustache without a beard was never an English fashion in the Middle Ages.)

Young men were often clean shaven, with the back hair to the nape of the neck only.

8. ACCESSORIES

The Girdle became more ornamental about 1150, and was tied like a sash in front with hanging ends [1170–90]; or, long and elaborate, was fastened with ornamental buckles [1175]. The purse was often attached to one hanging end.

Wallets or Pouches, varying in size from purses to 'handbags', varied also in shape and decoration; slung from either (*a*) the girdle, or (*b*) the breech girdle (also called the brayer); they were in the latter case hidden under the tunic.

Keys were usually slung from the brayer and so concealed.

Gloves only worn by men of rank, and then seldom. Gloves with jewelled backs were worn by kings, as shown by the effigies of Henry II and Richard I at Fontevraud.

Not before the thirteenth century were gloves worn generally in England.

Walking Sticks, plain or decorated, were rare.

Jewellery. Rings, brooches, buckles, clasps and ornamental fillets of gold or silver were worn by nobles.

Decoration of Garments. Embroidery continued to be fashionable.

Dagging (*c.* 1170–1500, but the height of fashion from 1380–1440), a crude form of vandyking, was used at this period for the lower edge of the hood gorget and sometimes round the bottom of tunic or super-tunic.

Materials. Leather, often with the hair left on and with that surface outside, was used by peasants for tunics and mantles.

Wool, linen and silk were also in use.

Twelfth Century

WOMEN

1. THE KIRTLE or GOWN

Worn over the smock, and corresponding to the male tunic, as in the previous century, and always with a girdle.

Sleeves plain and close fitting at first.

The new style [1130s–1170], appearing after the first quarter, was characteristic of the twelfth century, but worn by ladies of rank only. The bodice was moulded to the figure, fitting tightly down to the hips; below that level the skirt, cut to expand considerably, fell in many close folds to the ground, often spreading behind into a train. The bodice was frequently depicted with an all-over pattern suggestive of smocking; its method of fastening is uncertain; sometimes it seems to have been laced up, either in front or at the back. The round neck without decolletage, and the skin-tight fit, would make it impossible to put on the garment over the head. Occasionally the neckline was cut in a moderate V in front, especially with noble ladies, thus exposing the top of the smock.

The *sleeves* were tight fitting to below the elbows, where they abruptly expanded into long hanging cuffs often reaching the ground and appearing like 'streamers' dependent from the wrists. Sometimes these were bulged out below forming pouches. The streamers, and the skirt draperies, might be tied into knots to keep them out of the way.

The sleeves were sometimes of a different colour from that of the gown, green being popular.

2. THE GIRDLE

Extremely long and decorative, was either a thick cord of silk,

10. 12TH CENTURY

(a) Kirtle with pendant cuffs. Girdle tied in method (*b*) (p. 38). Mantle.
Hair in two plaits. Veil encircled with gold fillet. (*c*. 1170). (b) Kirtle
with pendulous cuffs. Girdle tied in method (*a*) (p. 38). Mantle fastened
with brooch. Crown over veil. (1140-60). (c) Super-tunic with pattern.
No girdle. Hooded cloak (*c*. 1170). (d) Cloak. Kirtle with pendant
and pouched cuffs. Gloves, unfingered, with long streamers. (*c*. 1150).
(e) Super-tunic with pendant cuffs. Hair in fouriaux (p. 40). (1130-50).

wool or linen, or was made of thongs plaited together or worked into a design on a broader belt ending in silk cords.

Methods of wearing:

(*a*) Passed round the hips to be tied at a lower level in front, the ends hanging down in midline almost to the ankles.

(*b*) Passed round the front of the waist and knotted or crossed over in the small of the back, then brought forward and downward and tied in front, the ends hanging in midline to the ankles.

N.B. The exaggerations of this style diminished during the second half of the century.

3. THE SUPER-TUNIC

Followed the pattern of the previous century, but was closer fitting, with a tendency to exaggerated length, drapery effects, and wider sleeves, which sometimes had pendent cuffs and could not be worn over a gown with similar sleeves.

Pelissons were worn by ladies of rank.

4. THE CLOAK and MANTLE

Similar to that of the eleventh century.

Hooded cloaks, probably for winter, were in common use towards the close of the century.

5. LEGWEAR

Stockings, gartered by woollen ties above or below the knees, continued in use.

6. FOOTWEAR

Shoes, as in the eleventh century.

7. HEADWEAR

(1) THE VEIL. As formerly; noble ladies always wore veils in public during the first half of the century.

(2) HALF BENDS (Bands) of gold, or complete circles such as

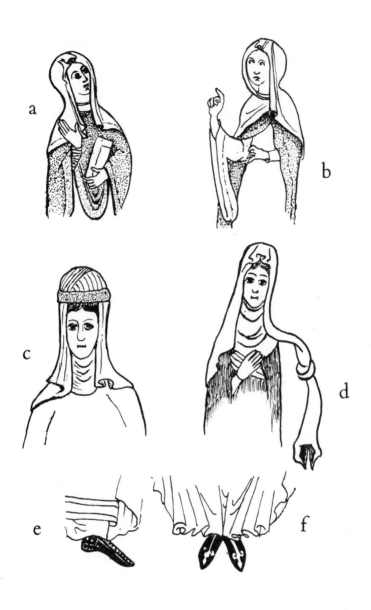

11. 12TH CENTURY

(a) Closed mantle. Open veil (*c.* 1155). (b) Open mantle. Open veil.
Pendulous sleeve. (*c.* 1155). (c) Fillet, wimple, open veil. (d) Scarf-like
veil, wimple. (e) and (f) Decorated shoes. [(c) to (f) 2nd half 12th c.]

diadems, were worn over the veil, helping to keep it in place. Queen's crowns were worn over the veil.

(3) A LONG NARROW BAND, passed round the head over the veil and knotted on one side, leaving long flowing ends, was sometimes worn during this period (c. 1130s–1170s) when streamers were fashionable.

(4) BARBETTE AND FILLET (late twelfth century to early fourteenth) consisted of a linen band passed under the chin to the temples, worn with a linen 'crown' encircling the head (see thirteenth century).

(5) THE WIMPLE OR GORGET (1150–1340, after which unfashionable, and in fifteenth century worn by widows only). Made of fine white linen or silk, was a neck covering draped over the bosom (often tucked inside the neck of the gown), and round the front of the neck; the ends, then drawn up to frame the face, were pinned to the hair above the ears or on top of the head under the veil which was usually worn as well. In later centuries the wimple generally covered the chin.

8. HAIR

Mostly concealed by veil and wimple or veil alone, the latter being the usual mode for all except the nobility. Young girls wore their hair uncovered, with a centre parting, the locks falling loose or curled on to the shoulders; or with one or two long pigtails, plaited or enclosed in a silk sheath ('*fouriau*'). This is usually depicted coloured white with red circular stripes.

New style for those of very high rank [1120–1150]. The hair, parted in the middle, was then braided into two long tresses which descended in front of the shoulders reaching sometimes to below the knees. The plaits were reinforced by false hair or tow and braided with ribbon, and the ends often tipped with ornaments. Or the plaits were encased in silk fouriaux. This style was usually worn with a loose flowing veil secured by a gold circlet or, in the case of a queen, by a crown.

9. ACCESSORIES

Elegant *Girdles,* as described.

Jewellery. Ornamental chaplets of gold, bracelets, rings, neck-laces and brooches.

Gloves rare, but occasionally worn by ladies of rank. Even gloves might have streamer-like cuffs, as depicted in Fig. 10 (d). In this case the gloves had thumbs but no separate compartments for the fingers (B.M. Cotton MS. Nero C IV. The miniature represents the Virgin with a pair of doves in her hands.)

N.B. *Rouge* was in general use by the higher ranks.

Thirteenth Century

MEN

1. TUNIC, KIRTLE or COTE

In addition to the former styles of short and long tunics, worn with a girdle, a new cut appeared, characteristic of this century. The *sleeves* were made in one piece with the body (as in magyar sleeves) leaving a wide armhole often extending to the waist; the sleeve being cut to slope off to a narrow tight cuff at the wrist. (End of twelfth century to end of thirteenth century.)

Both long and short tunics were now usually slit up in front as far as the girdle.

2. SUPER-TUNIC or SURCOTE (a term chiefly belonging to the thirteenth century).

The old style continued to be worn by the less fashionable, a girdle being optional.

New Styles

(1) TABARD variety, without sleeves. Consisted of a panel front and back, expanding downwards from the shoulders to reach calf level or lower. It was put on over the head, having a wide neck aperture, the panels being sewn together for a short distance at waist level, or fastened with clasps. It was also often slit up in front to the same level. No belt worn.

(2) The HERYGOUD, (13th and early 14th c.), like the contemporary French garde-corps, was a cloak-like garment down to the ankles or just below knees. Often made with wide tubular sleeves gathered at the shoulders and reaching well beyond the hands. For convenience the arm could be passed through a long vertical slit in the front of the upper part of the sleeve, which was

12. 13TH CENTURY

(a) Tabard, open at sides except near waist level, worn over long front-vented tunic. Soled hose. Spurs. Decorated gloves (*c.* 1270). (b) Sleeveless surcote (mid 13th c.). (c) Herygoud: hanging sleeves and hood; old-style tunic (mid-13th c.). (d) Long tunic with front slit and 'magyar' sleeves. Ceremonial mantle with jewelled clasp. Criss-cross leg bandages to above knees (high class) over soled hose. Stalked cap. Long gloves. (Early 13th c.).

left hanging loose. Put on over the head, it was generally hooded and could act as an outer garment for warmth.

Usually no belt was worn with it.

(3) A LOOSE SUPER-TUNIC, with short wide sleeves reaching just below the elbows, was occasionally worn. A belt, often buckled, was optional [1260–1360].

(4) The GARNACHE [1260–15th c.], reaching below the knees, was made like the Tabard type, but with shoulder line cut wide enough for the material to fall down to the elbows on each side, producing cape-like sleeves. Beltless. Often worn as a cloak over the surcoat. The sides were either

    (*a*) Joined just below waist level.

    (*b*) Sewn up from waist to hem.

    (*c*) Left open all down the sides.

(5) A SLEEVELESS SURCOAT with belt.

3. FITCHETS (First appeared *c.* 1250)

Vertical slits resembling pocket openings made in the super-tunics which had no side openings. Through them the purse or keys, slung from the girdle, could be reached, or the hands warmed.

4. CLOAKS and MANTLES

Unchanged. See also Herygoud and Garnache (above).

5. LEG WEAR

(1) STOCKINGS unchanged. Sometimes gartered below the knee with narrow strips of material.

(2) LEG BANDAGES for the nobility, with a criss-cross arrangement, reaching above the knees were worn for a short period. (*c.* 1200)

6. FOOTWEAR

(1) SHOES, shaped to the foot.

    (*a*) Plain, and mostly closed round ankle, with inner lacing, or sometimes buckled.

    (*b*) Open over foot and cut high behind the ankle, as in twelfth century to end of thirteenth century.

13. 13TH CENTURY HEADWEAR

(a) Small hat with knob on crown. (b) Hat with round crown and rolled brim. Also shows short sleeve of super-tunic. (c) Coif. (d) Hat slung on shoulders. (e) Hat worn over coif. (all 1250s)

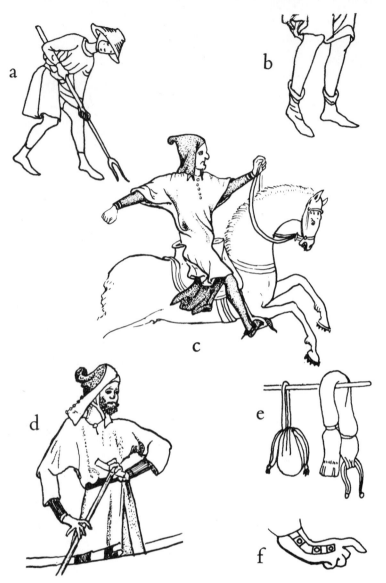

14. MID-13TH CENTURY

(a) Peasant in front-vented tunic, straw hat, fitting boots. (b) Short loose boots. (c) Garnache (?) with short neck-fastening. Long cote. Open hood without gorget. Soled hose, pointed. Spurs. (d) Boatman in front-vented surcote, 'magyar' sleeves. Hood open, showing lining and buttons. Coif. (e) Two purses. (f) Decorated glove.

(c) Open over foot and closed by ankle or instep strap.

(2) BOOTS, or Buskins. Coloured tops for a brief period. All now had a much looser fit. Many barely reached the calf.

7. HEADWEAR

(1) THE HOOD, often without gorget, sometimes buttoned.

(2) THE STALKED ROUND CAP like a beret, as in twelfth century.

(3) THE LARGE BRIMMED TRAVELLING HAT, as in twelfth century.

(4) HAT WITH BROAD BRIM turned up at the back; occasionally worn reversed with turn-up in front.

(5) HAT WITH ROUND CROWN, sometimes with a knob on the crown, and a moderate brim with a downward slope; or a rolled brim or a hat like a small bowler.

(6) THE COIF (end of twelfth century to 1440) continued in use and was much in evidence.

8. HAIR

Worn with centre parting or a fringe, and waved to nape of the neck. Beard and moustache of moderate length only, as compared to previous century. Young men had 'bobbed' hair with straight or waved fringe, or a roll curl across the forehead. A similar curl was sometimes worn at the nape of the neck, and this always escaped from the coif if worn. The face was clean-shaven in young men.

9. ACCESSORIES

As in the twelfth century.

Gloves, worn by the highest rank, were either long, reaching nearly to the elbows, or wrist length.

These were often decorated with a broad strip of gold embroidery down the back as far as the knuckles. (Edward I was buried with jewelled gloves). Individual glove makers are mentioned in Colchester records in 1295.

Gloves began to be more widely worn towards the end of the century.

Buttons, gilded or silver, were used as ornaments.

Thirteenth Century

WOMEN

1. THE KIRTLE or GOWN (also called Cote).

Worn with a girdle, and similar to the simple garment of the twelfth century, but the neckline tended to be slightly lower; or it was made with a short V opening which was closed at the throat with a brooch. These gowns remained very long with full draperies and trains.

Sleeves, fitting or loose. The tight sleeves were sometimes laced.

Fitchets (appeared first *c.* 1250), as in the male garment, were made in the woman's kirtle at the end of this century, implying that sometimes the purse was slung from a sash round the smock.

2. THE SURCOAT

(*a*) A voluminous garment with long massive draperies. Put on over the head through a wide neck opening. The sleeves, ending between elbow and wrist, expanded to a wide aperture (first half of thirteenth century). Subsequently they were closer fitting.

No girdle worn as a rule.

(*b*) The sleeveless surcoat, similar but without sleeves, the armhole consisting of a long vertical slit (Fig. 18a). Neck opening often wide from side to side, producing the effect of shoulder straps.

3. THE PELISSON

A super-tunic lined with fur, as previously worn.

48

15. 13TH CENTURY

(a) Surcoat (embroidered) with kirtle sleeve emerging. Crown over
veil. Mantle. (b) Fur-lined mantle over kirtle with girdle. Veil worn
open. (Late 13th c.)(c) Trained kirtle with typical 13th century 'magyar'
sleeves. Gold circlet and loose hair of young girl.

Furs. Fox and squirrel were the fashionable kinds; the commoner sorts were rabbit, cat and hare.

4. CLOAKS and MANTLES

Very long, and often trained, as in twelfth century.

Occasionally hooded, for travelling, and used to end of fourteenth century.

Mantles for the higher ranks were made of silk lined with fur. These were sometimes used as *dressing gowns,* e.g. Henry III gave his sister Isabel 'two scarlet cloaks, one lined with fur, the other with silk, to be used when she rose at night'.

5. STOCKINGS

As in the twelfth century.

Henry III ordered three yards of bruneta cloth worked with gold to make stockings for his sister.

6. FOOTWEAR

Shoes, as for men.

7. HEADWEAR

(1) THE VEIL, as before, or long and scarf-like.

(2) THE BARBETTE AND FILLET. Typical of the thirteenth and early fourteenth centuries. Worn without the veil.

The barbette was a linen band passed under the chin and pinned on the top of the head. It often broadened considerably at the angle of the jaw, sometimes giving it a coif-like appearance.

The fillet was a stiffened linen circlet varying in width from a narrow band to a broad crown with a slight outward splay. *Goffered Fillets* were common [*c.* 1250] though this decoration was used earlier.

Gold circlets or coronets were worn inside the fillet by noble ladies.

The shape of the fillet changed to accommodate itself to the changing hair styles, and later became broadened from side to side, instead of being circular.

16. 13TH CENTURY

Surcoat with fairly close sleeves and kirtle sleeves to wrist. Mantle much draped and cord hanging loose in front. Wimple, veil and fillet. (*c.* 1269).

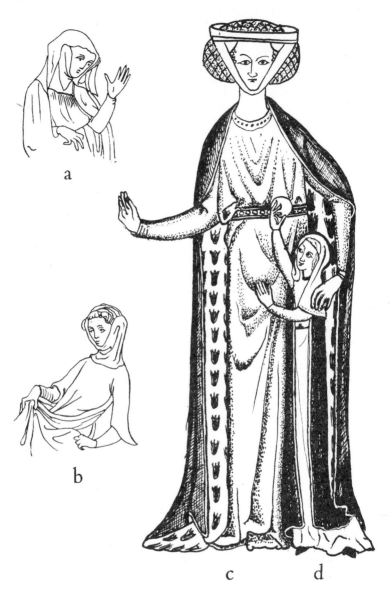

a

b

c   d

17. 13TH CENTURY
(a) Veil and wimple (1350–1400). (b) Wimple alone, pinned up (1350–1400). (c) Fur-lined mantle, kirtle with 'magyar' sleeves. Barbette and fillet over fret (net). (d) Little girl in kirtle without fashionable sleeves. Plain cloak, simple veil.

The hair was turned up at the neck and pinned to the barbette, or enclosed in a net or *fret*. This hair net confined the hair under the barbette and fillet, and was never worn alone except by women of the lower class.

Garlands or *chaplets* of flowers or of goldsmith's work were worn by young girls.

(3)   *The Wimple* continued to be worn; this with the veil, or the veil alone, might be worn with a fillet.

Veils and wimples were sometimes dyed yellow at the end of the century.

> *Wymples, kerchyves, saffrund betyde*
> *Yellugh under yellugh they hyde.*
>
> (Robert of Brunnes *Handlyng Synne,* 1303)

8. HAIR

Almost invisible throughout this century.

(*a*) Turned back from the forehead and twisted or plaited into a roll at the back of the head, and covered with the net.

(*b*) Later [1270] from a centre parting it was rolled or plaited on each side of the face over the ears, and above these side plaits, which were usually covered by the net, the widened fillet was fitted.

9. ACCESSORIES

Gloves, of fine linen, were worn by ladies of high rank to protect their hands from sun-burn.

Jewellery. Gold chaplets, bracelets, rings, necklaces and ornamental buttons.

When Princess Eleanor attended her sister's wedding in 1290, she wore a dress 'adorned with 636 silver buttons'. (*The Wardrobe and Household of Henry, son of Edward I.* Hilda Johnstone. Manchester University Press, 1923.)

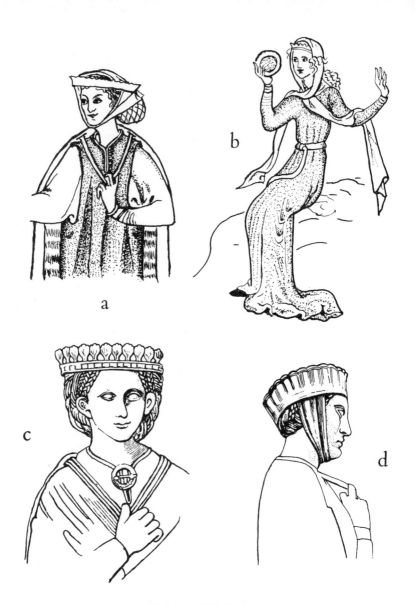

18. 13TH CENTURY

(a) Mantle, fur-lined, held by its cord which passes through slots (to ornamental bosses on the outside). Fillet broad from side to side, barbette, hair-net (mid 13th c.). (b) Young girl in kirtle with train. Veil scarf-like. Hair loose (mid 13th c.). (c) Coronet. Hair plaited over ears and twisted up behind. (d) Barbette and goffered fillet. (1230-60).

First Half of
the Fourteenth Century

MEN

The styles of the late thirteenth century persisted through the first half of the fourteenth, and, unfashionably, until near the end.

During the *first quarter,* long ceremonial garments, e.g. tunics and super-tunics, were retained.

During the *second quarter* a break from the traditions of the past became noticeable, with fashion moving towards better cut and producing garments of closer fit revealing the shape of the body. At the same time men's clothes became steadily shorter, exposing the legs in long tight-fitting hose.

Buttons, hitherto mainly decorative, came to be widely used as practical fastenings though preserving an ornamental character in gold, silver, brass, copper, crystal, glass, as well as silk, damask and hair.[1]

1. THE SHORT TUNIC

This, sometimes slit up in front and with sleeves of the magyar (for a few years) or plain form, continued in use by the lower classes. It was worn with a girdle, and sometimes shortened to hip level revealing the braies; but the tunic was rapidly going out of fashion, being superseded by

2. THE GIPON, POURPOINT or DOUBLET (replacing the tunic) 1335.

The name 'doublet', though used in France at this period, did

[1] Mrs. Russell-Smith has found evidence that buttons were used as fastenings in the 13th century and even by the Romans.

19. 14TH CENTURY, MAINLY 1ST HALF

(a) Peasant's tunic with front slit to skirt, showing long stockings with button fastening, also garter, Ankle shoes. (b) Gipon, and ankle strap shoes (1352–62). (c) Gipon buttoned all down front, hood thrown back (mid 14th c.). (d) Gipon with belt, looser, more like a tunic. Hood with short liripipe. Garters and decorated shoes. [(a) and (d) *c.* 1340].

not become a general term for the civilian garment in England until the fifteenth century.

The Gipon, replacing the tunic, was worn over the shirt, being a close-fitting, slightly waisted garment, falling without folds or gathers to just above the knees. Its bodice was padded, usually throughout.

Fastened all down the front by lacing or a close row of ball or flat buttons [1335]. With the less fashionable, buttoned to waist only.

The *neck* was low and round [1335–1420].

Sleeves tight to the wrist, the fit obtained by a row of buttons matching the rest, from elbow downwards.

> *Botones azur' d wor ilke ane*
> *From his elboth to his hand.*

[from a MS. in the British Museum (Cotton Collection).]

A *girdle* was rare, as the gipon was usually covered and the belt confined to the cote-hardie. During the second half of the century, however, when the gipon was frequently worn without the cote-hardie, then a belt was essential.

3. OVER-GARMENTS

(1) The COTE-HARDIE of the gentry [1330–1450].

This replaced the super-tunic and was worn over the gipon. It was low-necked and tight-fitting, buttoned or laced down the front to waist level whence it flared into a full skirt open in front and reaching to the knees.

The *sleeves*, ending at the bend of the elbow in front, expanded abruptly behind into a short tongue-shaped hanging flap, varying in length and breadth. The flaps, even the sleeves, could be absent.

Its *girdle* or belt was usually worn below waist level.

(2) The COTE-HARDIE of the lower classes was looser and frequently without front fastening; put on over the head through a wide opening which was often then narrowed by folding over the material in front and presumably pinning it.

The *skirt,* ankle or knee length, was generally slit up the front to the girdle or short of it.

The *sleeves* resembled those of the more fashionable garment.

20. 14TH CENTURY, 1ST HALF

(a) Cote-hardie with exaggerated sleeve flaps. Hood with liripipe. Ankle shoes. (b) Long cote-hardie, showing buttoned gipon sleeves. Fur-lined mantle. Decorated ankle shoes. (c) Garnache with tongue-shaped lapels, over old-fashioned super-tunic and tunic. Large country hat with strings, worn over hood. Large loose buskins. (d) Cote-hardie taken off over the head. Old-fashioned tunic. (All *c.* 1340).

21. 14TH CENTURY, 1ST HALF

(a) Hood with liripipe twisted round head. Short tunic. Thigh length boots, buckled below calf. (b) (c) (d) Garnaches. (e) Peasant in short tunic showing braies. (f) (g) Men in hoods, two in fur shoulder capes; short boots. (All *c.* 1340).

The *girdle* or belt worn (*a*) at waist level;

(*b*) at the fashionable level;

(*c*) not worn. With this style fitchets were frequent.

(3) THE GARNACHE continued as in the thirteenth century, the length reaching to mid-calf or ankle. Sometimes long-sleeved. The neck opening had a feature characteristic of the fourteenth century, namely two small *tongue-shaped lapels* at the neck, of a paler shade than the garment itself and sometimes furred. The lapelled form was apparently called a *houce* in France (Boucher *et al.*)

(4) The loose short-sleeved, or sometimes sleeveless, SUPER-TUNIC persisted, the latter sometimes slit up in front from hem to thighs.

(5) THE TABARD: rare except for heralds' wear (Cf. Fig. 66(c)).

(6) MANTLES were, as previously, long ceremonial garments.

4. OUTER GARMENTS

(1) THE CLOAK, usually long, circular in cut, was fastened in front or buttoned on the right shoulder. Costly linings were fashionable among the nobility.

(2) SHOULDER CAPES [1330–1430] independent of hoods, were worn.

(3) CAPES WITH LOW COLLARS, cut on the circle, reaching to mid-thigh and closely buttoned down the front. Some had hoods.

5. LEGWEAR

HOSE OR STOCKINGS

(*a*) Knee length, ending just below the joint.

(*b*) Thigh length, reaching well above the knee.

(*c*) Socks reaching to just below the calf; frequently decorated with circular bands e.g. red and white [*c.* 1340].

Soled hose, i.e. with a thin leather sole attached and worn without shoes or boots, continued in use to the end of the fifteenth century.

Decoration of hose. Often of different colours from the main garment, or different from each other; or one leg might be

22. 14TH CENTURY, 1ST HALF

(a) Peasant with stirrup-hose turned down over garters; sheepskin cloak closed at neck, open each side. (b) Soled hose (striped red and buff) with spur. (c), (d) and (g) Types of shoe. (e) Boot (bent over spade) with horizontal thong fastenings. (f) Similar boot, outer surface. All early 14th c. [(a) (d) (e) and (f) c. 1330].

divided vertically into two different colours. This arose from the widespread custom, all through the fourteenth century, of nobles having garments embroidered with heraldic motifs, producing parti-coloured effects from the mixed colour schemes.

Garters. Strips of wool or linen, often embroidered, tied below the knee, the ends tucked in or left dangling, used for long or short stockings.

Long stockings were sometimes also attached by being buttoned at the thigh, possibly to a string from the braie girdle.

6. FOOTWEAR

(1) SHOES

(*a*) Well cut and shaped to the foot with a point at the big toe; fitting round the ankle and laced on the inner or outer side, or else with a flap folding across a long tongue.

(*b*) Cut away over instep (like a slipper) and fastened round ankle by strap and buckle.

In the higher ranks shoes were decorated by being embroidered or punched into patterns (squares, dots or flowers).

(2) BOOTS or BUSKINS

For riding some were shaped up to the thighs and fastened by buttons, laces or buckles below the calf; others were loose and unshaped, made to fit the leg by means of a front fold which was buttoned or hooked down the outside of the calf. For walking, *short boots*, side-buttoned or laced, were common.

'To Robert le Fermor, bootmaker of Flete Street, per six pair of boots with tassels of silk and drops of silver-gilt, price of each pair, five shillings, bought for the King's use. Westminster, 24 May. £1 10s.' From Wardrobe Accounts of Edward II in 1321.

For a peasant's boot see Fig. 22(e) and (f). Even for work these were thin soled.

7. HEADWEAR

(1) THE HOOD continued in use, but developed a *liripipe,* i.e. an extension of the point of the cowl into a hanging tail. The liripipe (1330 to 1450 and on hats to 1480) was long or short, and (with rare exceptions) was always made in one piece with the

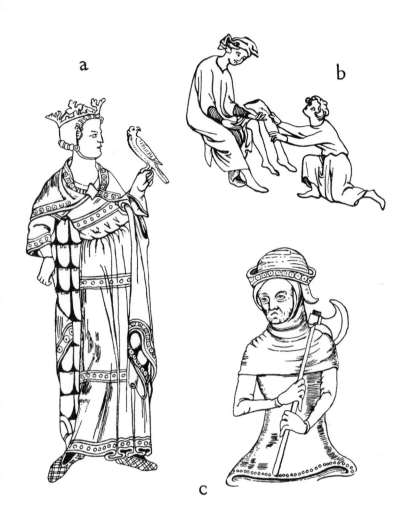

a

b

c

23. 14TH CENTURY, 1ST HALF

(a) Ceremonial fur-lined mantle over long embroidered surcote. Embroidered ankle strap shoes. Crown worn over coif. Hawking glove. (c. 1325). (b) Man in hood worn turban-wise (p. 65 example (d)) putting on long stockings. (c. 1320.) (c) Hat worn over hood with short liripipe. (c. 1340.)

24. 14TH CENTURY, 1ST HALF
HEADWEAR

(a) and (c) Hats with brims peaked in front, turned up behind; (c) has pilgrim's badge, the scallop shell. (b) Stalked round cap. (d) Stalked 'beret'. (e) Large travelling hat with fastening cord, worn over hood. (All *c.* 1340).

hood. If cut vertically it would hang on one side or the other; if cut horizontally it would hang down the back. The long liripipe would often be twisted round the head turban-wise. The liripipe was very rarely lined.

Materials for hoods. Generally cloth lined with same material; sometimes with fur; rarely with taffeta.

The lining was sometimes of a different colour from the hood; sometimes this distinction was given only to the face piece.

An embroidered band round the lower border of the gorget was common.

(2) HATS

(*a*) Thirteenth century styles continued, mainly worn by country folk, the stalked beret being very common.

(*b*) A hat with a small round or domed crown, the wide brim turned up sharply behind and forming a peak in front.

(*c*) A high domed crown or round 'bowler' shape, either having a rolled or close turned-up brim (1325 to end of fifteenth century).

(*d*) A turban headgear made from the hood. The face opening was drawn over the head and turned up into a rolled brim, leaving the point of the hood and the gorget to flop over in opposite directions. This became the fashionable 'hood turban' of the next period [1340-1380].

(3) THE COIF continued to be worn.

8. HAIR

Styles of the thirteenth century continued in fashion, with a clean-shaven face, though sometimes beards with or without moustaches but without side whiskers, were worn, e.g. 'these bearded bucks' (Robert of Brunne). The roll curl across the forehead and at the nape of the neck, with a clean shaven-face, was very prevalent.

9. ACCESSORIES

The *Girdle* or Belt became very ornamental, often being tied in front or buckled, the long ends hanging loose.

25. 14TH CENTURY, 1ST HALF . HEADWEAR

(a) (c) (d) Hoods worn turban-wise with facial opening fitting the head (p. 65 example (d)). (b) (f) Hoods with long liripipes (b) also shows cote-hardie and hawking glove. (e) (h) Hats with round crowns and (e) close turn-up brim, (h) rolled brim. (g) High hats with domed crowns and rolled brims, worn over hoods. Note that (d), a carver, wears a primitive apron. [(c) beginning of 14th c., the rest c. 1340].

26. 14TH CENTURY, 1ST HALF. ACCESSORIES

(a) Pouch and dagger at belt. Hood slung over shoulder. (b) Peasant with particoloured mitts, one tucked into his belt. Hose gartered at knee. (c) Shepherd. Hood with gorget rolled up. Hat slung behind. Boots buckled or buttoned. Mitts. (d) Peasant's mitts. (e) Cup bearer wearing fringed napkin. (f) Server using napkin as waiter's gloves. (c. 1330, all the rest c. 1340).

The *Dagger* was slung vertically from the belt on one side, or suspended from a cord tied to the belt, or fastened to the back of the pouch.

The *Pouch* was also slung from the belt by two straps, and carried by all classes.

The *Penner* and *Inkhorn* were similarly slung from the belt.

Gloves, all made with a spreading gauntlet cuff, were universally worn, often merely carried in the hand, by all classes. Those worn by nobility were embroidered, by labourers often had separate thumb and first finger, the other three fingers being in one compartment. Made of coarse thick materials. 'The glovers of London were recognised as a separate organisation circa 1349' (Linthicum).

Aprons were worn by carvers, cooks and butchers.

Spurs were worn by civilians as well as by men in armour. They were strapped to the ankles, often over soled hose, not boots, and from 1300 onwards were fitted with a rowel instead of a simple spike. See p. 46, Fig. 14c; p. 61, Fig. 22b and p. 145, Fig. 66c.

First Half of Fourteenth Century

WOMEN

1. THE KIRTLE or GOWN

Continued at first unaltered.

But by 1330 this, with the Cote-hardie, had changed fundamentally. Instead of concealing the shape of the body it revealed the feminine contours, being cut to mould the figure to the hips, whence it expanded abruptly and fell in widening folds to the ground.

The neck was low, sometimes baring the shoulders, a startling innovation to some contemporaries. 'A gown open thus at the neck seems like the hole of a privy' (From MS. of 1300 to 1310).

The sleeves were tight and long, either buttoned from elbow to wrist or sewn up. 'To render her vesture more perfect a silver needle was filled with a thread of gold, and both her sleeves were closely sewed' ('*Roman de la Rose*').

The kirtle was *fastened* by front or back lacing from neck to waist, or just below.

The girdle, (optional) was worn round the hips and might be exposed to view through the side openings of the sleeveless surcoat.

2. OVER GARMENTS

(1) THE COTE-HARDIE [1320–1450], worn by women over the kirtle, and similar in cut to those of the men, being close-fitting, low-necked and long. Either buttoned down the front to below the waist (as with men's), or made with a low neck and put on over the head.

27. 14TH CENTURY, 1ST HALF

(a) Sleeveless surcoat over kirtle. Apron. Hood open in front; small
liripipe. (b) Pouch at belt. (c) Cote-hardie. Veil and fillet. (d) Apron
over kirtle. (e) Sleeved surcoat over kirtle. Closed veil. (All. *c.* 1340).

a

b

c

28. 14TH CENTURY, 1ST HALF

(a) Kirtle. Barbette and fillet. (b) Sleeved surcoat. Veil and wimple
[(a) and (b) *c.* 1320]. (c) Herygoud.

Sleeves elbow-length, expanding into small or large tongue-shaped hanging flaps.

Fitchets, i.e. the vertical placket holes in the skirt, were fairly common.

No girdle worn.

(2) THE SLEEVED SURCOAT, loose and unshaped, continued in use. It was sometimes made with side vents.

Length: (*a*) To the ground, or
(*b*) Sometimes just below the knees.

Sleeves with wide expansion below elbows.

(3) THE SLEEVELESS SURCOAT continued in use, occasionally slit up at the sides for a short distance above the hem.

No girdle.

3. OUTER GARMENTS

(1) SHORT PELISSONS.

(2) CLOAKS. Long full and hooded, worn for warmth when travelling.

Mantles with costly linings, and loosely tied with tasselled cords springing from jewelled attachments, were ceremonial.

(3) THE HERYGOUD was occasionally worn by women as an outer wrap [Fig. 28(c)].

4. STOCKINGS

Unchanged. Gartered above or below the knees.

Materials, wool or linen, and coarse wool for the poor.

5. FOOTWEAR

Shoes in the style and decoration used by men.

6. HEADWEAR

(1) VEILS AND WIMPLES continued to be worn in the former style.

(2) VEILS ALONE, or secured by a fillet placed low on the head, began to be arranged thus: The veil was pulled into the shape of the head (coif-like) and securely pinned in place, leaving two

29. 14TH CENTURY, 1ST HALF

(a) Mourning hood worn at funeral (*c.* 1330). (b) Open hood with small liripipe over open (coloured) veil (*c.* 1340). (c) Sleeveless surcoat. Veil moulded over hair bosses, flowing ends. Wimple. Hawking glove. (d) Woman carrying baby in wrappings bound with swaddling bands. (e) Boy in beltless tunic, hood thrown back. Soled hose [(c), (d), (e) *c.* 1320].

long ends to fall behind as streamers. When no fillet was worn the hair, enclosed in a net, might appear at the temples.

(3) THE BARBETTE AND FILLET continued in use during the early years of the century, usually worn with a fret, and occasionally draped with a small veil.

The barbette was now frequently fixed over the head outside and not under the hair net.

The fillet was usually fairly shallow.

The fret (or hair net) was often brightly coloured e.g. red with white spots.

(4) FRET AND FILLET (without barbette). The fret was brought well down over the hair, which was massed in coils round the ears; the fillet, worn low, crossed the upper part of the forehead. 'More than half a basinfull of pins' used to secure these headdresses.

(5) HOODS were now worn by all for travelling and warmth, and by country women at all times. Worn covering the face at funerals.

Liripipes were short or long.

Women's hoods were always open in front, and therefore not put on over the head like men's. For warmth the gorget might be folded across the neck or buttoned up from hem to chin. Hoods were often worn over another head-dress, such as veil and fret.

7. HAIR

Plaited and coiled round the ears on each side, and usually covered by the fret or completely hidden by veil. This arrangement produced projections or, in contemporary language, 'bosses' on either side of the face.

Vertical plaits hugging the cheeks were fashionable from 1340 to 1400. A narrow fillet with rigid vertical strips to support the plaits, was common.

8. ACCESSORIES

Aprons worn domestically and by country-women. Usually large, without bib, and tied round the waist. A band of

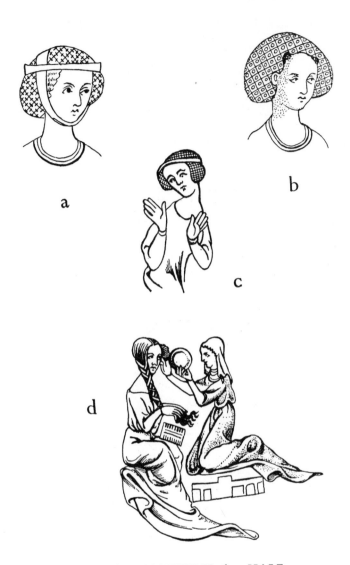

a

b

c

d

30. 14TH CENTURY, 1ST HALF
HEADDRESSES

(a) Fret, barbette and fillet. (b) Fret alone. (c) Fret and fillet. (d) Hair-dressing—coiling a plait above the ear. Lady inspecting result in mirror. (All *c.* 1340).

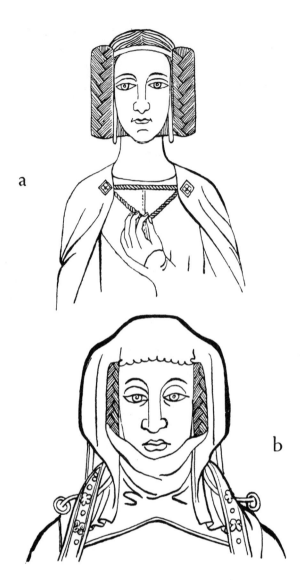

a

b

31. 14TH CENTURY, 1ST HALF
(a) Vertical plaits, with supporting side pieces from fillet. (1384. Style 1340-1400.) (b) Vertical plaits partially covered by veil and wimple. (1349).

embroidery along the upper border, below the waist belt, was very common.

Gloves worn by all classes.

Jewellery. Rings, brooches, buckles, etc. as for men.

Heraldic motifs, and even short mottoes, were embroidered on ceremonial cloaks, as with men's.

A CONTEMPORARY DESCRIPTION of tournaments, tempus Edward III, is appended. 'These tournaments are attended by many ladies of the first rank and greatest beauty, but not always of the most untainted reputation. They are dressed in particoloured tunics, one half being of one colour and the other half of another, with short hoods and liripipes which are wrapped about their heads like cords; their girdles are handsomely ornamented with gold and silver and they wear short swords or daggers before them in pouches, a little below the navel; and thus habited they are mounted on the finest horses that can be procured and ornamented with the richest furniture' [Henry Knighton's Chronicle written *c.*1360 (Translated from the Latin)].

Second Half of the Fourteenth Century

MEN

1. THE GIPON (called DOUBLET for civilian use by 1370s).

Continued to be tight-fitting, waisted, and buttoned or laced down the front, except for working men [Fig. 33, compare (d) with (a)].

The changes were:

(*a*) Extra padding in front, giving a 'pouter-pigeon' effect.

(*b*) The skirt grew steadily shorter, scantily covering the hips; and was usually joined by a seam to the body. Short side vents that could be buttoned were sometimes present.

The sleeves, still tight and buttoned from elbow to wrist, or sewn up. (Chaucer speaks of 'with a threde bastynge my sleeves', using 'a sylver nedyl'.)

New Variations

(*a*) Sleeves, usually extending to the knuckles, expanding into a funnel shape.

(*b*) The 'grande assiette', a form of sleeve much rarer in England than (*a*). This was cut so that the sleeve was inserted with a circular seam overlapping the front and back of the bodice, plate-wise.

The Neck remained low and round until *c.* 1420. A standing collar followed.

Estaches, i.e., strings, were now sewn to the under surface of the gipon below for the attachment of the hose, formerly suspended from the girdle of the braies (drawers).

The gipon, especially during the last quarter of the fourteenth

78

a

b

32. 14TH CENTURY, 2ND HALF

(a) Gipon with ornamental buttons, sleeves buttoned from elbow to knuckles, knightly girdle. Dagged mantle buttoned on right shoulder. Long hose. Ankle shoes with inner lacing. (*c.* 1350). (b) Cote-hardie with long tippets. Shoulder cape. (*c.* 1350).

century, was sometimes worn without an over-garment, in which case it was belted.

2. THE COTE-HARDIE

The changes were:

(*a*) The front fastening extended from neck to hem.

(*b*) The sleeves were fairly close fitting to the elbow; the hanging flap became longer and narrower, and was known as a '*Tippet*'. French 'Coudière'.

(*c*) The Tippet was a straight band of material, generally white, which hung down to the knees or lower. Usually a similar white band encircled the sleeve forming a cuff at the elbow.

(*d*) The length rapidly diminished like that of the gipon, and the cote-hardie skirt was often dagged.

(*e*) During the last quarter of the fourteenth century the cote-hardie, still closely buttoned down the front, developed a collar.

Just at the close of the century long sleeves, buttoned down the forearm and expanding into a funnel shape over the hands, came into fashion. The garment gradually became almost indistinguishable from the short Houppelande (which see for description), with similar varying sleeves and collar shapes. But the belt of the cote-hardie was worn round the hips; that of the houppelande was worn round the waist.

The buttoned front of the cote-hardie ceased about 1400, when pleats usually hid the fastenings, which were probably hooks and eyes.

From 1390 to 1410, the cote-hardie was worn extremely short, ending at the fork, a fashion favoured by the 'exquisite', though not by others.

The *girdle* was worn over the cote-hardie round the hips, and was often very ornate and long.

The knightly girdle [1350–1410], worn by nobles over the cote-hardie, was a broad belt of highly decorative metal plaques joined together and fastened in front by an ornamental buckle.

33. 14TH CENTURY, 2ND HALF

(a) Peasant in tunic-like, but short, doublet. Hose. Overstockings
rolled at knee and soled. Straw hat. (1377-99). (b) Similar, but strap
shoes in lieu of overstockings. (c) Gipon horizontally quilted (p. 100).
Hood. Buttoned cape. (c. 1350). (d) Gipon very waisted, padded over
chest. Ornamental belt. Hood dagged, buttoned, with long liripipe.
Soled hose with pointed feet. (c. 1360).

Always worn at hip level, and therefore probably sewn or hooked on.

3. THE GARNACHE

Its use continued, usually with the small tongue-shaped lapels at the neck, characteristic of the French *houce*.

4. THE HOUPPELANDE (1380 to 1450, after which known as the Gown). The name given to a new type of gown, a characteristic upper garment from 1380 and throughout the following century.

General description:

All made on the same principle, varying only in detail. Narrow above, steadily expanding downwards; thus fitting the shoulders but falling below into gradually deepening tubular folds which were kept in place at the waist by the belt. It was cut from four pieces, with a seam front and back and one on each side. These seams were often left open for a short distance from the hem, making *vents* in front, behind, and at the sides, the number varying according to fancy [1380–1440].

Length: (a) Long, to the ground (ceremonial).

(b) Short, knee length.

(c) Any intermediate length.

The Neck had a very high upright collar expanding like the neck of a carafe and reaching to the ears or higher behind, sometimes merging with the headgear.

Its edge, often closely dagged, gave a marked resemblance to a ruff. The collar was hooked or buttoned in front from chin to chest. Very occasionally it was fastened behind, or the top buttons in front were left undone and the collar partially turned down.

This gown was put on over the head.

Towards 1400 it was sometimes buttoned all down the front.

Sleeves. Funnel shaped, widening from the shoulders downwards and ending in an immense aperture, the lower edge sometimes reaching the ground. The upper edge never fell beyond the wrist, leaving the hand free. Sleeves frequently dagged.

Dagging (or Jagging) (used after 1170, widely fashionable from 1380 to 1440 but continued off and on to 1500).

This form of decoration, now extremely fashionable and complicated, consisted in cutting almost any border of any garment into elaborate scallops in the shape of leaves, tongues, fringes and compound vandykes, sometimes added as appliqué work in overlapping series. It was particularly applied to the houppelande, being used for the hem, up and down the slits of the skirt, round the huge sleeve opening, and very fully round the top of the collar, producing the ruff-like effect already mentioned.

Epaulettes, dagged and embroidered, were very common.

'May not a man see as in our days the sinful costly array of clothing, and namely in too much superfluity ... that maketh it so dear, to the harm of the people, not only the cost of the embroidering, the disguising, indenting or barring, ounding (waving), paling, winding or bending, and suchlike waste of cloth in vanity; but there is also the costly furring in their gowns, so much pouncing of chisel to make holes, so much dagging of shears, with the superfluity in length of the aforesaid gowns, trailing in the dung and in the mire, on horse and eke on foot, as well of man as of woman.' (Chaucer, 'The Parson's Tale'.)

CEREMONIAL MANTLES continued.

5. OUTDOOR GARMENTS

(1) CLOAKS continued in use to the end of the century, after which they ceased to be fashionable, but were chiefly worn for travelling. The poor wore a short cloak (Chaucer's "*courtepy*").

(2) SHOULDER CAPES [1330–1430], usually heavily dagged, continued in use.

(3) CAPES, thigh length, cut on the circle, with low collars and closely buttoned down the front, also occurred at this period.

6. LEGWEAR

HOSE reached the fork. Round the upper border were pairs of eyelet holes, through which strings (French 'estaches'), from the under side of the gipon, were threaded and tied in a single bow.

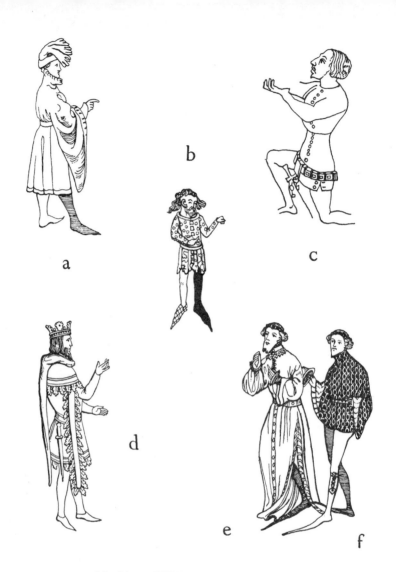

34. 14TH CENTURY, 2ND HALF

(a) Short fur-lined houppelande; high collar; rear vent. 'Hood-turban'
head-dress (p. 87 (2)). Parti-coloured soled hose. (Late 14th c.) (b)
Dagged gipon. Parti-coloured hose and shoes. (c. 1374). (c) Gipon with
side vents. Knightly girdle. (2nd half 14th c.) (d) Cote-hardie with
dagged tippets. Dagged shoulder cape. Hood thrown back; long
liripipe. (2nd half 14th c.) (e) Long houppelande with side vents.
(c. 1395-96). (f) Short houppelande. Piked soled hose. (c. 1395-96).

Hose were made of a stretchable material cut on the cross with a seam down the back.

Parti-coloured hose were common until 1420.

'... their hose are of two colours, or pied with more, which they tie to their paltocks (i.e. gipon) with white lachets called herlots.' (Anonymous author of *Eulogium Historiarum ... A History from the Creation to 1366.* [Late 14th c.] Translated).

Joined Hose, appearing at the very end of the century, are described in the next section.

The shape of the 'feet' followed the anatomical outline, but the point opposite the big toe was slightly increased.

Long exaggerated pikes [1395–1410] (i.e. pointed toes) appeared at the end of the century, the toes being stuffed with tow, moss or hay.

Soled hose continued in use.

7. FOOTWEAR

(1) SHOES. Similar to those of the first half of the century.

(*a*) Fastened by lacing on inner or outer side with close fit round ankle.

(*b*) With buckled ankle strap and short or long uppers.

Towards 1360 they began to be sharply pointed, and punched out designs were popular. 'Paule's windows carven on his shoes' (Chaucer[1]). Though not seen in contemporary illustrations, a fashion for long piked shoes was attempted but did not become established until about thirty years later. 'No knight under the estate of a lord, esquire or gentleman, nor any other person, shall wear any shoes or boots having pikes or points exceeding the length of two inches, under the forfeiture of forty pence; and every shoemaker who shall make pikes for shoes or boots beyond the length stated in this statute shall forfeit for every offence the sum of forty pence.' (Sumptuary law, Edward III).

In 1395 *Piked Shoes* or (Fr.) '*Poulaines*', with long spear-like points, came into fashion. The higher the rank the longer the points, both for the gentry and their attendants [1395–1410, revived later].

[1] Miller's Tale, Canterbury Tales.

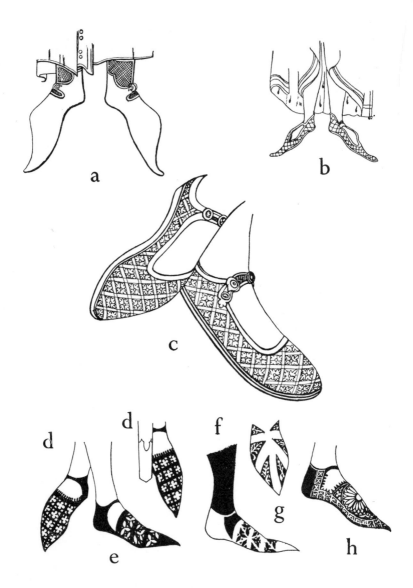

35. 14TH CENTURY, 2ND HALF

(a) Shoes with long uppers and buckled ankle strap (1376). (b) (c) Shoes with low uppers and buckled ankle strap. [(b) *c.* 1378]. (d) to (h) Shoes with long uppers, ankle straps, long pointed toes, punched out designs.

(2) BOOTS and Buskins, similar to those of the first half of the century, followed the piked fashion to a less degree.

Short Boots for walking, were laced or buttoned as in the first half. Hooked on the outer side (*c.* 1395) was a new method of fastening.

(3) GALOCHES or Clogs.

(4) PATTENS, wooden soles with leather straps, began to be worn with shoes to raise the foot from the ground in muddy weather (For description see p. 111). 'Their shoes and pattens are snouted and picked' [*Eulogium Historiarum*, late 14th c. (Trans)].

8. HEADWEAR

(1) THE HOOD with liripipe, as formerly.

(2) THE 'HOOD-TURBAN', a descriptive name only, for a new way of wearing the hood which entirely changed its appearance (1380–1420. Very common 1390–1410). The *facial opening* was now fitted on to the head, the edges rolled back, and the liripipe, if long, twisted round the crown, an end dangling on one side.

The *gorget* fell in folds to the opposite side, or if of stiff material it stood erect, in whole or part, fanwise above the head. Its edge, generally dagged, gave it a marked resemblance to a cock's comb. There were many variations of this according to taste.

Materials as formerly.

(3) The COIF continued in use.

(4) HATS.

The various styles of hat worn in the first half of the century persisted, but tended to become more decorative by added trimming. Two new styles emerged in the last decade (1) The padded roll, usually dagged. (2) The bag-shaped crown. Both are described in the next period, when they were common.

(*a*) *Plumes* began to appear, mostly of dyed ostrich or peacock feathers. One or two were fixed upright in front or behind, being attached to the base of the crown by a brooch or jewelled ornament. 'In none of the old romances, replete as they are with descriptions of dress and armour, is there any allusion to feathers earlier than the middle of the fourteenth century' (Planché's *Cyclopaedia of Costume*).

36. 14TH CENTURY, 2ND HALF
HEADWEAR

(a) (b) (c) Diagrammatic representations of conversion of hood.
(a) Hood; (b) hood with facial opening for head, and (c) final result,
producing—(d) (f) 'Hood-turbans' with liripipe twisted round head.
(e) High crowned plumed hat (*c.* 1378). (g) Bag-crowned hat worn
over dagged hood. (h) 'Hood-turban'. Early houppelande (End 14th c.)

(b) *Hat bands* with decorative designs became popular.

Materials for hats. Felt, beaver, or any showy textile.

Hats were sometimes slung behind by attached strings. 'His hat heng at his back down by a las' (Chaucer).

9. HAIR

Either

(a) From a centre parting the hair hung down to the upper or lower part of the neck.

or

(b) Hair cut fairly short all over, without a parting.

Face clean shaven, or beard and moustache, usually without side whiskers.

10. ACCESSORIES

Knightly Girdles.

Daggers.

Pouches.

Jewellery, such as gold head-circlets.

Gloves, for all classes.

Handkerchiefs. The word handkerchief is not met with until the sixteenth century. Previous to that period it was called '*hand cloth*' or *hand-coverchief,* or mokador. Their origin attributed to Richard II, e.g. 'little pieces of material made for giving to the lord King for carrying in his hand to wipe and cleanse his nose' (John Hervey's *The Plantagenets*).

Note on Mourning

About the middle of the fourteenth century black became more generally recognised as the symbol of grief.

Previously one dark, drab garment would be worn over ordinary coloured clothing or a hood worn over the face, as in Fig. 29(a), p. 73.

Second Half of
the Fourteenth Century

WOMEN

1. THE KIRTLE or GOWN

Continued with close-fitting bodice and full skirt, and girdle worn low.

> *He seeth her shape forthwith all*
> *Her body round, her middle small.*
>
> JOHN GOWER

Sleeves were tight-fitting to the wrist, and there expanded like mittens over the hand as far as the knuckles. Buttoned from above or below elbow to hand (1330 to end of Middle Ages).

2. OVER GARMENTS

(1) THE COTE-HARDIE continued as in the first half of the century, but the short flaps hanging from the tight elbow sleeves changed to long streamers or *Tippets*. These were similar to the men's except that, like the garment itself, the tippets were always very long, often trailing on the ground. No girdle was worn unless the cote-hardie replaced the kirtle immediately beneath the sideless surcoat.

(2) THE SIDELESS SURCOAT (1360 to 1500; ceremonially up to 1520) was an important and characteristic garment from now to the end of the Middle Ages. It developed from the sleeveless surcoat. Its distinguishing feature was the large side openings stretching from shoulders to hips. They extended low enough to reveal the underlying *knightly girdle* or ordinary belt, whichever

37. 14TH CENTURY, 2ND HALF

(a) Sleeved surcoat with fitchets. Kirtle sleeves emerging. (*c.* 1370.)
(b) Cote-hardie with fitchets; long tippets to sleeve (*c.* 1364). (c) Sideless surcoat with plackard; side opening shows girdle of kirtle. (1378–80.)
(d) Sideless surcoat, and 'chaplet' head-dress. (*c.* 1380.)

was worn. The gap was often wide enough to leave only a narrow strip of material down the front.

A *Plackard* was the name given to the front portion forming a stomacher curved in to the waist, and usually rounded below giving a variation in form. It was sometimes made of fur.

From the hips this surcoat hung in loose folds to the ground.

The *neck* was low and wide, the garment being slung from mere shoulder straps. To prevent its falling off there is some evidence that it was fastened at the waist behind the plackard to the gown beneath. Its *decoration* comprised a row of buttons or jewels down the midline in front. *Fur borders* and lining were usual. 'In the summer it were better away entirely because it only serveth for a hiding place for the fleas' (Knight of La Tour-Landry. *Book for Instruction of his Daughters* (1371-72. Translated).

(3) A LOOSE SLEEVELESS SURCOAT, sometimes having side vents, was still worn as a domestic style or by the poorer classes.

(4) A LOOSE, SLEEVED SURCOAT, without a girdle, continued. It might be buttoned from top to bottom down the front (1380s). Low necks were fashionable.

(5) MANTLES, chiefly ceremonial, long and much decorated, were loosely fastened across the chest by jewelled bands or tasselled cords. These mantles were sometimes parti-coloured and embroidered with heraldic devices (see Fig. 53, p. 123).

3. OUTER GARMENTS

(1) HOODED CLOAKS, for travelling or riding (Ladies rode side-saddle; countrywomen astride).

(2) SHORT PELISSONS continued in use.

4. STOCKINGS

Reaching above the knee, and gartered above or below.

> *Here hosen weren of fine skarlet redde*
> *Ful straite y-teyed.*

Chaucer's description of the wife of Bath, *Canterbury Tales.*

5. FOOTWEAR

SHOES as for the men, but never with long pikes.

a

b

38. 14TH CENTURY, 2ND HALF

(a) Kirtle with front lacing. Low girdle. Long mantle. Goffered veil; the so-called 'nebula' head-dress. (c. 1370.) (b) Sideless surcoat showing plackard and kirtle belt on her left. Side plaits supported on extensions from coronet. (c. 1388.)

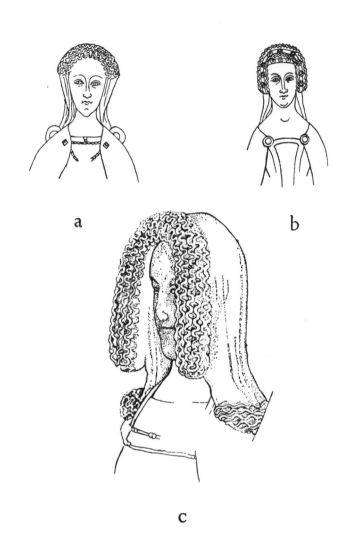

a

b

c

39. 14TH CENTURY, 2ND HALF
HEADWEAR

(a) Goffered veil, ruched only round forehead. (c. 1393.) (b) Goffered veil worn over fillet. (c. 1391.) (c) Goffered veil, the ruching forming an arch round the face. (c. 1370.)

6. HEAD WEAR

Veils and *Wimples* continued, but more ornamental veils began now to appear.

(1) The GOFFERED VEIL or NEBULA HEADDRESS [1350–1420], descriptive names assigned later. Made of a half-circle of linen, draped over the head. Possibly several layers were used at times. The straight edge, decorated by a *broad goffered frill* resembling a ruff, formed an arch round the face, ending at the temples or descending to the chin or below. Thence it was continued ungoffered, to meet the circular border which draped the shoulders. The latter might be goffered also in whole or in part.

The goffered 'arch' was sometimes square, covered with ornamental network, and worn over a fillet which was visible in front only across the forehead.

(2) An ORNAMENTAL FILLET, with attached side-pieces resembling carved or openwork pillars hugging the cheeks in front of the ears, gave the face a very square shape. These side 'pillars' were hollow, a tress of hair being drawn through each. The rest of the hair was covered by a fret or a veil which hung down at the back.

Coronets, when worn, were usually shaped to fit over the side pieces.

(3) An ORNAMENTAL FILLET, or CORONET WITHOUT SIDE PIECES. Worn with fret or veil as in (2), or very occasionally without either. But a vertical plait of hair was fixed in position on each side of the face, in place of the 'side pillars'.

Head-dresses (2) and (3) gradually merged, at the end of the century, into the more elaborate structures of the next century, built upon the same principle.

(4) 'CHAPLET HEAD-DRESS' [1380–1415] a *padded roll* worn over a hair net; a fashion appearing near the close of this century and typical of the next.

(5) HOODS and HATS continued in use for homely wear or for travelling.

(6) FRETS or HAIR NETS, also known as CAULS, were very usual with all types of head covering. 'A fret of golde she hadde next her heer' (Chaucer, *Legend of Good Women*).

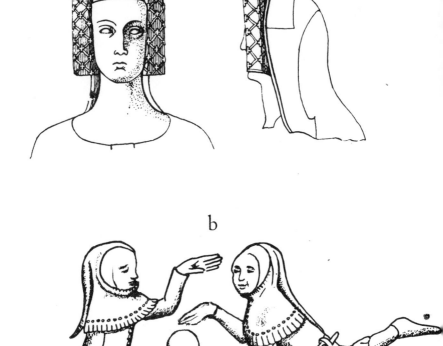

40. 14TH CENTURY

LATE HEAD-DRESS. YOUTHS' COSTUME

(a) Front and side view of head-dress, showing ornamental network covering goffered veil. Fillet worn outside veil. (b) Gipon fashionable in having conspicuous buttons, tight body and dagging, but suitable for youth in having full skirt. Hood dagged, with long liripipe. Pouch and dagger at belt. (Mid-14th c.).

7. HAIR

As formerly, coiled, braided or crimped round the ears, partly concealed under fret or head-dress, if not hidden under the veil.

Fashionable ladies, from 1340 to 1400, often arranged their hair in vertical plaits which were passed straight down in front of the ears from the fillet to the angle of the jaw, and sometimes held in place by a net. The ends were turned up and hidden under the head-dress.

Shaved front hair, to produce a broad high forehead, was a new mode [1370–1480].

The hair was frequently dyed saffron colour.

Eyebrow plucking and face painting became fashionable [1370–1480]. '. . . fair daughters, see that you pluck not away the hairs from your eyebrows nor from your temples nor from your foreheads, to make them appear higher than Nature ordained'. (Advice to his daughters by the Knight of La Tour-Landry, 1371–72).

8. ACCESSORIES

As for the first half of the century.

Jewellery very abundant. A richly clad woman was:

> Icrouned with a coroune, the King hath no betere.
> All here fyve fingris were fretted with rynges
> Of the purest perreighe [gems]
> (Piers Plowman (c. 1369–70) ed. Knott and Fowler 1952).

Knightly girdles.

Decorative effects were becoming more marked; a variety of colours were in use, especially green.

Dagging was less frequent on women's garments.

The *fashionable Posture* for women was to thrust forward the abdomen with the back curved, producing a 'slouching' attitude.

First Half of
the Fifteenth Century

MEN

1. THE DOUBLET.

From 1400 to 1670 the term "doublet" was used, for what corresponded to the gipon. 'I be-quethe to Richard my servant . . . and a doblet' (will of John Solas 1418). Worn over the shirt as a tight-fitting, well waisted garment; clinging to the hips it barely reached to the thighs. It was padded throughout with extra thickness over the chest. Made up in eight pieces, with a centre seam down the back and a seam round the waist. It was rarely worn uncovered after 1412.

Belted at hip level when worn alone.

Fastenings: (a) By lacing down the front [1400–1450].

(b) By buttons or hooks and eyes [after 1425].

The Neck

(a) Continued round and collarless for 15 to 20 years [to 1420]

(b) Then collars were added [1420–1490], being close-fitting, and (from 1450 to 1490) stand-up, with a V opening in front, cut with points under the chin, sometimes laced across.

Sleeves

(a) Close-fitting to the wrist, extending to the knuckles, and buttoned up to the elbow, the buttonholes being placed as near the edge as possible and the buttons having long shanks [1360–1420].*

(b) 'À grandes assiettes' (see fourteenth century, second half) [1360–1440].

The doublet was now supplied with pairs of *eyelet holes* round

* Ending at the wrist from 1420 on.

98

a

b

c

41. 15TH CENTURY, 1ST HALF

(a) Long houppelande, buttoned down chest; tubular sleeves; doublet sleeves emerging. Shoulder belt for dagger. Hood thrown back. Instep strap shoes. (*c.* 1400–5.) (b) Long houppelande, buttoned throughout. Belt knotted and buckled. Buttons to mantle, and hood thrown back. (*c.* 1400.) (c) Houppelande, lined and edged with fur; standing collar with V opening. Front vent to skirt. Bagpipe sleeves. High shoes with inner lacing. Bowl crop hair. (*c.* 1437.)

the hem corresponding to similar pairs round the upper border of the hose; the latter were attached to the doublet by ties called *points* threaded through these openings (See section on Hose).

Materials. For ordinary use: broadcloth, linen, fustian, sometimes leather.

For special occasions; damask, satin or velvet. Mixed materials were employed when the doublet was mostly hidden by the gown, e.g. body of plain material with collar and sleeves of a more ornate stuff. (Commonest from 1430 to 1460).

Quilting

The lines of stitching were:

(*a*) Vertical (usually military).

(*b*) Horizontal (usually civil).

(*c*) Invisible (also civil), having a flat surface, the quilting confined to the lining.

2. THE COTE-HARDIE (Sometimes called a Jacket).

Still close-fitting and very waisted, but now often made with gathers in front and behind.

Fastened invisibly, probably hooked behind under the pleats.

Length. Very short, at first barely reaching the fork (among the ultra-fashionable, 1390 to 1410). Knee length [1410–1450].

Neck. At first a high stand-up collar [1380–1420].

No collar after 1420, when this was transferred to the doublet.

Sleeves

(*a*) Close-fitting with bugle cuffs reaching the knuckles; buttoned to elbows.

(*b*) Other sleeves resembling those described under 'Houppe-lande' (*q.v.*) into which the short cote-hardie merged.

Belt worn at hip level.

3. THE HOUPPELANDE, or Gown.

Though essentially the same in structure, it now showed many changes in detail. If there were no vents [1440–1550] it was called a *"closed gown"*, although open in front. It was fastened

42. 15TH CENTURY, 1ST HALF

(a) (b) Short houppelandes, with closed hanging sleeves. [(a) 1400-1416, (b) c. 1440]. (c) Ditto. Third man wearing one sleeve normally. Short boots with outer lacing and pattens. (c. 1440.) (d) Houppelande with hanging sleeves having no opening at wrist. Hood with liripipe twisted round the head. The man holds a falconer's lure. (c. 1433).

down the front from neck to hem by buttons or more often by hooks and eyes, mostly concealed under folds which were stitched down into place under the belt.

Fitchets were very occasionally present.

Arrangement of folds

(*a*) Eight folds were the commonest (two in front, two behind, and two at each side) [1410–1440].

(*b*) Like massed organ pipes, front and back, for the whole length, with plain smooth sides [1440 on].

The Neck

(1) With Collar [1380–1425].

(*a*) Very tall 'bottle neck' collar, usually dagged, buttoned up to the chin from chest. Sometimes this style was closely buttoned from chin to hem, contrary to the usual custom [1380–1410].

(*b*) The same shape, but lower, and having a V opening at the throat [1400–1425].

(*c*) A large turned-down collar spreading flat over the shoulders [1410–1425].

(*d*) A very low upright collar with rounded edges sloping to a wide V in front, resembling the doublet collar which showed above it [1425–1460].

This fashion overlapped that of no collar.

(2) Without Collar (1425 to 1500. Rare earlier in England.).

The neckline varied, but was generally edged with fur regardless of the season.

(*a*) Fitting in front and sloping to a V behind [1420–1480].

(*b*) Fitting in front and sloping to a U behind [1450–1470].

(*c*) Fitting behind and sloping to a V in front [1430–1465].

(*d*) Sloping to a V in front and behind (off and on).

(*e*) Round neck [1425-1500].

Sleeves

Three types: open, closed or hanging (open or closed).

(1) Open Sleeve

(*a*) An immense funnel-shape, as previously described (1380 to 1420. Ceremonially up to 1450).

(*b*) A plain cylindrical sleeve of equal width from shoulder

43. 15TH CENTURY (1st half)

(a) Short houppelande with 'closed' hanging sleeves. Neck ornament.
Doublet collar appearing above. (*c.* 1429.) (b) Very short houppelande,
bag-pipe sleeves and high dagged collar. (1408.) (c) Very long ceremonial houppelande, wide funnel-shaped sleeves. Round neck with
doublet collar rising above it. (*c.* 1415-20.)

to wrist; largely worn by peasants, but became fashionable
c. 1430 [1400–1500].

(c) A short sleeve which was in effect the cylindrical sleeve
rolled up to the elbow level, giving a cuff-like appearance,
especially as the lining was usually of a different colour
(1400 off and on to 1480s).

(2) The Closed Sleeve (1405 to 1500. Occasionally seen up to
1520.) This was very full, and cut in one piece with a seam down
the front, and buttoned at the wrist. It might be gathered or
plain at the shoulder; gathered into a wristband or shaped to the
wrist without a cuff; or any combination of the two.

Variations:

(a) *The Bagpipe Sleeve,* also called the *Pokys* (1400 to 1430s.
Very popular c. 1410). Enormously wide, and shaped to form
a hanging bag or pouch, and often used as such. 'May rightly
be called the Devil's receptacles for whatever could be stolen
was popped into them' (Gough, Vol. 1 p. clxiii)[1].

(b) Much less full, but gathered to form a 'kick-up' at the
shoulder, and gathered below into a wristband [after 1445].

(3) Hanging Sleeves

All had an opening in the form of a slit down the front of the
upper part, allowing the arm (in its doublet sleeve) to be passed
through at will.

(a) The closed variety, full and gathered or shaped into a
cuff [1400–1520s], being much commoner during the first half
of the fifteenth century. A rare type had no opening at the
wrist, and resembled a hanging balloon, a German mode
which spread to France and England [1430–1435].

(b) The open variety, the sleeve being long and cylindrical.
Decoration of Houppelande

(a) Fur borders to neck, hem, vents and wrists were characteristic of this period, and were used all the year round
[1420–1515]. After 1515 these borders were largely relegated
to ecclesiastical vestments.

Fur linings common in winter.

The furs used, in order of popularity, among the wealthy:

[1] Full titles of reference books are given in the Bibliography.

44. 15TH CENTURY, 1ST HALF

(a) Long houppelande, wide funnel sleeves, hat with bag-shaped crown
(c. 1392). (b) Huke, belted round front panel, the back hanging loose;
bordered with oblique bands (c. 1450). (c) Huke, belted round both
panels; fur-edged (c. 1450). (d) Huke, unbelted. Chaperon with liripipe
worn like a scarf; gorget hanging behind (c. 1433). (e) Houppelande
(gown), fur-bordered, low waisted. Chaperon with '*burlet*' only (p. 113).
(c. 1433).

sable, ermine, civet, beaver, grise, fox and lamb. Ermine studded with black tails was reserved for royalty.

The poorer classes used hare, coney, cat and red squirrel.

(b) Dagging

(c) Embroidery

(d) Woven patterns in damask or figured velvet:

(i) Dotted patterns of circles, stars, wheels, roses or asters [common 1400–1450].

(ii) Trailing designs, usually very massive. All colours were used [very common c. 1430].

Materials for Houppelandes

Wool, velvet, satin, damask.

Linings

In summer. Satin, silk, taffeta, linen or plain cloth.

In winter. Fur or cloth.

Houppelandes were rarely unlined.

Thomas Occleve protests it was '. . . an evil to see one walking in gownes of scarlet twelve yards wide, with sleeves reaching to the ground, and lined with fur worth twenty pounds or more. . . . The taylors must soon shape their garments in the open field for want of room to cut them in their own houses; because that man is best respected who bears upon his back, at one time, the greatest quantity of cloth and of fur.' [*Regement of Princes*, 1412 (paraphrased)].

4. THE BELT

This was essential all through the first half of the fifteenth century. A symbol of degradation was to deprive a man of his belt. Very rarely, and as a sign of humility, a beltless gown was worn.

Position

(a) At waist level [1400–1500].

(b) Sometimes below [1400–1460].

Materials. Leather or spun silk coloured (black, white, green, blue, vermilion and other shades).

Buckles for fastening belt. Often richly worked, of gold, silver, iron or copper. In shape oval, oblong or square; single commoner than double. Usually worn centrally in front, but could be placed on either side of midline.

Some belts were tied in a knot after being buckled, and some had a long hanging end reaching to mid-calf [1400–1425. Very common *c.* 1425].

Objects slung from the belt

(*a*) Purse or pouch of leather of varying designs.

(*b*) A knife or dagger; often fixed to the back or the front of the purse; when no pouch was worn the dagger was hung by a sling or small chain fastened to the belt at any position.

CEREMONIAL MANTLES continued.

5. OUTER GARMENTS

(1) THE CLOAK went out by the middle of the century.

(2) THE SHOULDER CAPE, usually dagged, worn independently of the hood [1330–1430. Off and on later].

(3) THE HUKE [1400–1450. Rare later]. Originally worn over armour, became a civilian garment, replacing the cloak for outdoor wear. Worn over the gown in winter and over the doublet in summer, was of tabard design, and put on over the head. Generally belted, and occasionally sleeved.

Two types:

(*a*) The *riding huke,* short, reaching to mid-thigh; slit up in front for convenience in the saddle.

(*b*) The *pedestrian huke;* knee-length or a little longer; no front slit.

N.B. The huke of ground length came in during the second half of the fifteenth century.

6. LEGWEAR

Two types of hose: (1) Separate like stockings. (2) Joined, combining stockings and breeches in one garment, like modern 'tights'.

(1) SEPARATE HOSE

Though far less common these were never entirely discarded;

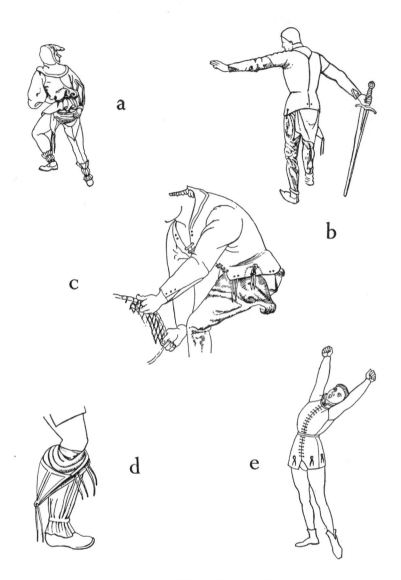

45. 15TH CENTURY, 1ST HALF

(a) Tongued separate hose with points which have given way. (b)
(c. 1452) and (c) show also eyelet holes in doublet, and points trussed
and untrussed. (d) Labourer's separate hose, footless and gartered at
knee and ankle, points undone. (e) Doublet, laced down front. Joined
hose with codpiece, and neatly trussed with points (c. 1430).

worn especially by labourers and inferiors. Made very long, with a top edge round or tongued for easier attachment to the front of the doublet. The upper border was pierced with eyelet holes through which strings were threaded and then passed through similar holes in the doublet. These, acting as suspenders, were called '*points*' or '*herlots*'. The procedure was known as 'trussing the points'. (See section on Joined Hose).

Points being very apt to break, labourers used few, especially at the back, or none at all, and instead rolled down their hose below the knee. In summer peasants working in the fields discarded their hose, wearing shirts and braies only.

Short hose, gartered below the knee and occasionally footless were also worn by labourers.

(2) JOINED HOSE (1400 to 1515, after which the design changed).

These became inevitable with the wearing of shorter garments. The long legs, reaching to the fork, were united, and continued upwards over the hips forming 'tights', which at first barely covered the seat; reaching the waist by the end of the century.

They were fastened to the doublet, now very short, by *trussing* the points; the lower border of the doublet was pierced by eyelet holes in pairs corresponding to similar pairs round the top of the hose. The strings ('*points*') were tipped with ornamental metal tabs ('*aiglets*'), which were threaded through these holes and tied in a single loop. This style of doublet was often called a *paltock*.

Points were usually of leather. 'The inventory of a London haberdasher, 1378, listed a gross of "poynts of red leather", the earliest noted reference.' (Linthicum) (Double bows were never made).

Arrangement of eyelet holes in doublet and hose: All through the century the numbers varied from two to twelve pairs, the commonest being nine (Two pairs in front, three at each side, one pair behind).

The *Codpiece* [1408–1575], was a small pouch formed by a front flap at the fork, fastened by ties (Cod, an old term for bag).

Both separate and joined hose might be:

(*a*) Footed

(*b*) Stirrups only

(*c*) Without either (rare)

(*d*) Soled (worn without shoes), pattens being added in wet weather

The other forms were worn with shoes or boots.

Shape of the feet

(*a*) Piked, having long points, the ends stuffed with tow, moss or hay [1395–1410].

(*b*) As the shape of the foot, or rounded toes, later becoming pointed again [1410–1460].

(*c*) Return of long points ('piked') [1460–1480].

Materials

Hose were usually lined in part, and made of woollen material often reinforced with leather. 'Pair of hose of black kersey.' 'Pair of hose bound with leather.' 'Black hose vamped with leather.'

Colours

Often very bright. Parti-coloured hose were less popular in England than in France, and uncommon here from 1420 to 1470.

7. FOOTWEAR

All without raised heels.

(1) BOOTS OR BUSKINS

(*a*) *Short buskins* [1400–1500], reaching to calf, close-fitting (rarely, loose and baggy), fastened by lacing, buckles, or hooks and eyes, slightly to the outer side of the front midline. Made in one piece, with a seam down the back.

(*b*) *Long Buskins* [1400–1500. Commonest after 1450]. Reaching high up the thigh; only used on horseback until 1450.

Close-fitting, laced up on outer or inner side; a notch often made at the knee to facilitate bending the joint. Made in two pieces, the foot being joined to the leg.

Shape of foot, as for hose, i.e.

(i) Piked [1395–1410].

(ii) Natural shape, rounded or pointed toe [1410–1460].

(iii) Piked again [1460–1480].

Materials. Goat, sheep or cow-hide.

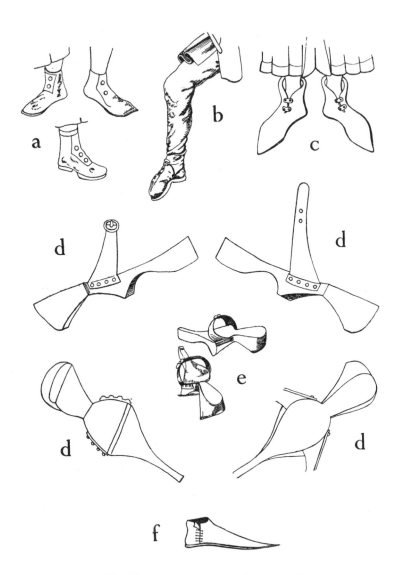

46. 15TH CENTURY, 1ST HALF

(a) Country shoes, one showing re-inforced heel and sole. (*c.* 1449.)
(b) Long riding buskin. (c) Buckled shoes. (*c.* 1460) (d) Pattens, side,
upper and lower views, diagrams of (e) Pattens (1434). (f) Piked shoes
with inner lacing (*c.* 1405).

Special Stockings were made for wearing inside the buskins and over the hose.

Leggings (or gaiters) bound by ties below the knee and round the ankle were worn by country folk.

(2) SHOES

All through the fifteenth century shoes were made like low boots, covering the foot and clasping the ankle, although open shoes fastened by ankle straps, of the fourteenth century style, continued in use for a few years.

Fastenings. Closed on inner or outer side, or down the centre by hooks, buttons, buckles, or lacing through eyelet holes (these *not* reinforced by metal). Frequently not fastened throughout, the portion round the ankle left gaping. Others were closed round the ankle, leaving a slit below to facilitate putting on the shoe.

Shoes were not indispensable, as soled hose, though usually worn indoors, were also worn out of doors.

Peasant's shoes were often reinforced with extra thickness at sole and heel.

Shape. As for boots.

(3) PATTENS [1400–1500. Known in 1390, but rare].

Worn with shoes, soled hose, and more rarely with buskins, to raise the wearer out of the mud.

Constructed with wooden soles, often raised at heel and toe, usually made of aspe[1] and painted white, shaped to the prevailing fashion of shoe but longer. Black leather straps were nailed on at each side (with four nails), and provided with buckles to fasten over the instep, or a 'saddle' over the instep secured them in position. Pattens were extremely fashionable from 1440 to 1460, and worn on all occasions indoors as well as out.

Leather pattens were occasionally worn by the nobility.

8. HEADWEAR

(1) THE HOOD [1160–1450, after which rare].

With closed gorget and long liripipe, and worn as a hood, continued for about 50 years. Small hoods, buttoned in front, and

---

[1] Aspe was used on account of its lightness. 'The most easy for wearing . . . of any timber that groweth'. (Linthicum).

47. 15TH CENTURY, 1ST HALF
HEADWEAR

(a) Hat, cone-shaped crown, brim turned up with an extra flourish in front. (p. 117 (i)). (Early 15th c.) (b) Hat with deep crown and divided brim turned up (p. 115 (h)). (c. 1416.) (c) (f) Hats with high crowns and rolled brims (p. 115 (a)). (c. 1400) (d) Chaperon with very long liripipe. Short houppelande with V opening in front (wide dagged sleeve unusual). (c. 1433.) (e) Peasant in small hat (p. 115 (c)). (c. 1416) (g) Chaperon with bias twist to burlet. No liripipe. (c. 1400).

usually worn thrown back forming a muffler round the neck, were now very fashionable. '... their hoods are little, tied under the chin and buttoned like the woman's, but set with gold, silver and precious stones' [*Eulogium Historiarum*', late 14th c. (Trans.)].

The *liripipe* on *hats* survived a little longer [till *c.* 1480]. It was occasionally used as a purse, the money being knotted in the closed end. The *liripipe* was sometimes *dagged* at this period [very common *c.* 1415].

The *hood-turban* continued in use (1390 to 1410, and unfashionably till 1420).

Materials and colours. Velvet, damask and russet. Black, green, purple, scarlet, blue and russet. 'Hood of russet velvet, with a tippet half of the same and half of blue velvet, lined with blue damask.'

'Hood of scarlet with a roll of purple velvet bordered with the same velvet.'

'Hood of russet velvet, the tippet lined with russet silk.'

'Hood of purple velvet without roll and tippet.'

'Hood of damask russet with tippet fastened with a lace of silk' (Sir John Fastolf's Wardrobe).

(2) THE CHAPERON (1420 to 1470, after which used by professions and older men). See Figs. 48a, b and 47g.

A characteristic feature. Developed from the hood-turban, which was inconvenient to adjust. The new form was a ready-made headgear, consisting of three parts stitched into place:

(*a*) The *burlet*, corresponding to the rolled facial brim, was a wheel-shaped pad stuffed with silk or cotton; either smooth and plain, or given a bias twist [common *c.* 1420] and, in this case, usually made with gorget but without liripipe.

(*b*) The *gorget* or *gole*, was now transferred from the neck to the crown of the head, where it was sewn inside the burlet and was long enough to form a capacious covering of two types:

(i) Sufficiently stiff to stand up, like a cock's comb sloping down from one side to the other (not from in front backwards). The 'tail' of the cock's comb overhung one side of the burlet, with the liripipe overhanging the other.

(ii) Limp, so that the bulk of the material hung down in

48. 15TH CENTURY, 1ST HALF

(a) Chaperon showing its three parts derived from the hood: gorget behind, liripipe in front, burlet (facial part) on crown of head. (b) Chaperon without liripipe. Forked beard. (c) Pilgrim's hat held on by cords passing through (?two) rings (cf. Fig. 49e). Scallop-shell badge of pilgrims' patron, St. James. (d) Wealthy man's hat. Ermine brim [(a) to (d) 1420–22]. (e) 'Hour-glass' hat on fashionable young man (1433). (f) Beaver hat with balloon crown.

folds over the side opposite to the liripipe, which served as a counter-weight to the gorget.

When no liripipe was present the folds hung down like a curtain round the back of the head, from ear to ear.

(c) *The Liripipe.* Chaperons (and, later, hats with attached liripipes) were frequently carried suspended over one shoulder (preferably the left) with the liripipe in front and the hat behind. Both chaperons and hood-turbans could be worn over a plain hood.

(3) A CHAPLET [1395–1410], resembling a burlet (but introduced earlier) and worn alone, was profusely dagged. It had the appearance of a wreath of closely packed leaves. Very popular and generally worn with a jewelled ornament in front.

(4) The COIF continued in use, but became gradually limited to the professional classes as part of a habit.

A *deep skull cap* made of various materials, not tied under the chin and usually exposing the ears, followed the coif for wearing under any other headgear [c. 1425 on].

(5) HATS

A vary large variety, many having very distinctive dates.

(a) A tall form of 'top hat', broadening from below up, and often but not invariably flattened from front to back, or from side to side. The brim turned up or rolled [1394-1415]. (Fig. 47f).

(b) A bag-shaped crown flopping forward or sideways over a rolled brim [1392-1430s]. (Fig. 44a).

(c) A low, tapering crown, with peaked brim turned up behind (thirteenth century to 1425). (Fig. 49d).

(d) A round crown with large turned-up brim [1410–1470].

(e) A round crown with brim turned down or rolled [1400–1500].

(f) A large ballooned crown with moderately wide brim turned slightly up or down. Very popular in England [1430–1460]. (Figs. 48f and 80c).

(g) A large hour-glass crown, sometimes with projecting spike on top, brim flat or turned up [1430-1440]. (Fig. 48e).

(h) A deep round or flat-topped crown with brim divided into front and back portions, both sharply turned up and

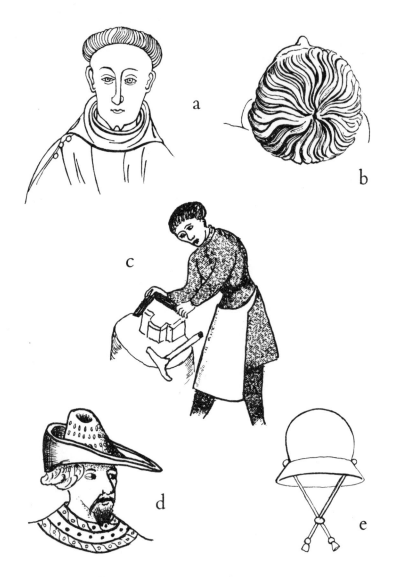

49. 15TH CENTURY, 1ST HALF

(a) Hair with bowl crop, wispy forked beard. (b) Top view of a bowl crop (*c.* 1446). (c) Mason in doublet, hose and apron. Bowl crop (*c.* 1425) (d) Hat with peaked brim and decorated crown. Decorated neck of houppelande. (1420–22). (e) Hat with strings, for travelling.

usually furred (Fig. 47b). Occasionally the back brim was turned down [1400–1440.]

(i) Tall cone-shaped crown with brim rolled or projecting and slightly turned up behind and down in front or vice versa [1445–1485]. Fig. 48d shows an earlier prototype.

Strings were used to tie hats under the chin when travelling (Figs. 48c and 49e), or to allow them to be slung on the shoulder.

Materials

Felt made from lamb, hare, rabbit or beaver; this last was the commonest, and was either rough or smooth. Beaver hats were usually lined with satin, cendal, velvet or scarlet cloth.

Straw hats were of various simple shapes.

Colours. Black, brown, grey, white or vermilion.

Trimmings

(a) Fur, very usual, the fur applied as a decoration to a felt body, often completely hiding the foundation.

The furs used were marten, miniver and astrachan.

(b) Plumes, hatbands, jewels, brooches and buckles.

9. HAIR

Early in the century to 1410 the hair was puffed out at the nape of the neck and on each side of the face, aided perhaps by pads.

The *Bowl Crop* (1410 to 1460, after which rather old-fashioned. Seen on tombs up to 1480), was extremely characteristic, becoming adopted almost universally. The hair was cut to resemble a shallow skull cap or inverted bowl with the rim only reaching to the upper level of the ears. Below this sharp line the head and neck were clean-shaven. The hair was brushed from a central spot on the crown to form a circular fringe round the head.

N.B. When long hair is shown in contemporary pictures it usually denotes imaginary characters; it was not a fashion in real life.

Short cropped hair was an unfashionable style appearing throughout the period.

Pointed or forked beards, with or without moustache, or a mere wisp of a beard, were worn early in the century, but rarely with

50. 15TH CENTURY, ACCESSORIES (1)
(a) SS collar, as worn (1418); (b) same, enlarged. (c) Ornamental
baldrick, jewelled (1485-90).

the bowl crop [1400-1415]. Later a *clean-shaven face* was the general rule, exceptions being rare [1415-1525].

10. ACCESSORIES

The Knightly Girdle [1360–1410] was worn at hip level over gipon or cote-hardie until 1410.

Jewelled Collars, often with personal devices, e.g. the 'SS collar' of the Lancastrians (1400 to 1550, but altered in design under the Tudors).

Folly Bells, an ornament composed of small bells hung

    (*a*) By chains from the girdle. (Cf. Fig. 70b.)

    (*b*) From a shoulder belt. (Cf. Fig. 70b.)

    (*c*) From a neck band.

Dagger and Pouch, as formerly.

Gloves, common to all.

Walking Sticks sometimes carried.

First Half of
the Fifteenth Century

WOMEN

1. THE KIRTLE

(Sometimes called by contemporaries a 'tunic', as in the trousseau of Princess Philippa, daughter of Henry IV.)

Worn next to the smock; was close-fitting, low-necked, with long tight sleeves sometimes reaching the knuckles like mittens, buttoned down forearm. The kirtle was buttoned or laced in front from neck to below waist or laced behind.

2. THE COTE-HARDIE

Continued as formerly till 1450, but was frequently hidden or replaced by the *Houppelande,* which became adopted by women in this country *c.* 1400.

3. THE SIDELESS SURCOAT (1360 to 1500, and to 1520 as state apparel and 1525 on effigies).

Continued unchanged to the end of the century, becoming then much less fashionable.

4. THE HOUPPELANDE or Gown [1400–1450s].

The Houppelande assumed the functions of a gown, during the fifteenth century.

This gown resembled the male houppelande in essentials; the minor differences being:

(1) The *belt* was worn at a high-waisted level.

(2) The gown was *always long;* on ceremonial occasions it

120

a

b

c

51. 15TH CENTURY, 1ST HALF

(a) Houppelande; high collar. Buttoned bagpipe sleeves. Kirtle sleeves emerging. Draped veil. (*c.* 1400.) (b) Mantle over kirtle, with buttoned sleeves extending to knuckles. Fillet. Templers above ears. Veil. (*c.* 1400.) (c) Houppelande with V neck and tubular sleeves. Veil draped over templers extending upwards and downwards. (1458 but typical earlier).

swept the ground, with a train of varying length. The hem might measure as much as twelve yards round.

(3) *The Neck*

(*a*) A tall decanter-necked collar, generally without dagging. The garment was usually put on over the head and buttoned up from chest to chin, though often left open at the neck, leaving a high V opening; or the top buttons were left undone and the collar turned down to decrease the height. Rarely the buttons extended down the centre from chin to hem [1400–1410, rarely to 1420].

(*b*) A broad flat turned-down collar, sometimes of fur, and a short V opening in front; or fastened by lacing from neck to chest [1408–1440].

(*c*) A wide V opening front and back, extending down to the belt; edged with broad revers narrowing towards the point of the V, leaving the neck bare, or revealing part of the kirtle or cote-hardie [1440–1460].

(4) . *Sleeves*

Similar to those of the male garment, but selective, e.g.

(*a*) Immense funnel-shaped; surviving a much longer period with women than with men [1400–1460].

(*b*) Plain tubular, of more or less equal width from shoulder to wrist [1400–1470].

(*c*) Bagpipe sleeve [1400–1430].

(*d*) Hanging sleeve of the open variety, being long and tubular. The closed variety was extremely rare, and the balloon shape unknown [1430–1500].

Loose Houppelandes, without belts and with closed necks, were sometimes worn by the elderly.

Ceremonial Mantles, long and full, cut on the circle; loosely fastened across the chest by tasselled cords or jewelled bands. Fur trimming along the borders was very common, and also fur linings.

'A mantle of blue cloth furred with pured miniver' (Trousseau of Princess Philippa, daughter of Henry IV 1406. *Archaeologia,* Vol. 67).

a

b

c

d

e

52. 15TH CENTURY (1st half)

(a) Elaborate fillet. Small templers. Bottle-neck collar of houppelande.
(c. 1410.) (b) Trained cote-hardie, long tippets from elbows. Kirtle
sleeves emerging. Chaplet head-dress over net. (Early 15th c.)
(c) Houppelande with flat collar and bag-pipe sleeves. Laced as far as
girdle. Veil draped over templers. (1432.) (d) Trained houppelande
with flat collar and trailing funnel-shaped sleeves. Wide padded roll
with short veil. (Early 15th c.) (e) Cote-hardie with short tippets.
Wired-up veil. (Early 15th c.)

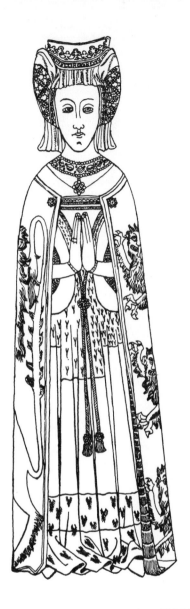

53. 15TH CENTURY, 1ST HALF

Fur-lined ceremonial mantle with heraldic motif*, fastened by long tasselled cord. Sideless surcoat trimmed ermine. Coronet shaped to fit over rising templers, draped with small veil. Elaborate necklace. (1446).

*The arms are those of the Powis family, of which this Lady Tiptoft was heiress.

a

b

c

54. 15TH CENTURY
EARLY HEAD-DRESS. PEASANT COSTUMES

(a) Veil over rising templers (1428). (b) and (c) Peasants in kirtles without overgarments, (b) with kirtle hitched up by girdle; old-fashioned hood and shoes, gypcière hung from girdle (1433); (c) Ale-wife. Kirtle short. Large bibless apron (?c. 1500. Head incomplete).

124

5. OUTDOOR GARMENTS

HOODED CLOAKS were still worn for travelling.

Some cloaks were buttoned in front with three or four buttons from chin to chest, and made with high collars to fit over that of the Houppelande, from 1400 to 1410.

6. HEADWEAR

THE HOOD (fourteenth century to 1450, after which continued for homely use, or mourning, to the end of the century). Continued to be worn for travelling and also by humbler folk. Worn open, some with projecting side flaps (Fr. 'oreillettes') standing out like ears from the sides of the face.

Hoods worn by the higher classes were often lined with fur. 'A hood of scarlet cloth and a hood of black cloth, both furred with miniver.' (Ibid.)

The *Liripipe,* for women's hoods, had sometimes a peculiar arrangement; being cut vertically it was then turned back and attached down the centre of the back of the hood so that at the bend two small pointed 'horns' projected.

New styles of head wear

During this century very elaborate headgear developed; these styles were thought far more decorative than the hair itself which, with certain exceptions, was not only concealed but often shaved off the forehead.

Breadth was emphasised during the first third of the century; then *height,* until about 1485 when a complete change took place.

The new styles may be classified into *Wide Shapes* and *High Shapes.*

(1) *Wide shape without side pieces (known as Templers or Templettes).*

The Chaplet or 'Cushion' head-dress was a thick padded ring of irregular shape, usually stretched out from side to side; often dagged, and generally trimmed with a jewelled ornament in front, as for men [1380-1410/15]. Worn over a net enclosing the hair, which was coiled above each ear so as to form a rounded mass each side (Fig. 52b). Heavy materials used for winter.

55. 15TH CENTURY, 1ST HALF
HEADWEAR

(a) Templers with narrow supporting fillet draped with veil. (1413.)
(b) Side view of templers and veil, also high houppelande collar left
open under chin. (c. 1410.) (c) Widow's veil and barbe. (c. 1446–50.)

56. 15TH CENTURY, 1ST HALF
Shows the goffering of a veil, draped over pointed templers (rare).
V neck, with revers, of houppelande. (1439.)

'A cap of beaver furred with ermine garnished with a silk
button and tassel' (Princess Philippa's Trousseau, 1406).

Light materials for other seasons. 'Five silk chaplets' (Princess
Philippa's Trousseau, 1406).

(2) *Wide shapes with Templers or French Templettes*

(*a*) The ornamental fillet or coronet, sometimes worn over
a net, had reticulated decorative bosses of goldsmith's work,
often jewelled. These bosses enclosing the hair at the temples,
were known as 'Templers' or 'Templettes'. The templettes ended

I 127

above the ears until about 1410–15. When pointed to c. 1440 but un-English. (Figs. 55a, 55b, 54a and 56).

'1 pair of templers 6/8' (Household Accounts of Queen Joan of Navarre 1419–21).

A fine gauze veil often worn under the fillet, directly over the hair, formed a hanging curtain behind [1400–1410–15].

(b) Fillet *with templers extending lower,* completely covering the ears and spreading outwards to a varying extent. The head-piece holding these structures was broadened in proportion, and the whole head-dress became more decorated and elaborate.

Veil optional but usual [1410–1430].

(c) The '*Horned Head-dress*' was an elaboration of (b) worn with a veil which was carried outwards beyond and above the side pieces on wires shaped like cow's horns [1410–1420].

(d) The '*Heart-shaped Head-dress*' was formed by curving the side pieces up into a U over the forehead; the circlet now fitted the temples and was hidden under the side-pieces.

The whole structure was usually draped with a small veil [1420–1450]. Compare Fig. 58a ('heart') with 59c ('horn').

(3) *High Shapes*

Worn without projecting side-pieces, and always with a backward tilt.

(a) A *Circular Roll,* sausage-shaped, was *bent up* on each side into a deep V over the forehead and back of the head. The gap at the sides was filled in now by part of the head covering (where formerly the side-pieces had been placed). The whole structure sat well above the ears with all the hair shaved up to its lower edge. A flowing veil was optional [1430-1480s].

To this type of headgear a gorget and liripipe were occasionally added as a decoration [1445–1460].

(b) A *Turban Head-dress* with an open crown circular or oval in shape, and placed well off the forehead, increased in height as time elapsed. Worn with or without a veil, which was occasionally replaced by the long hair flowing through or under the open top. Not common in England [1440s–1480s].

N.B. A V- or U-shaped loop placed in the centre of the shaved

128

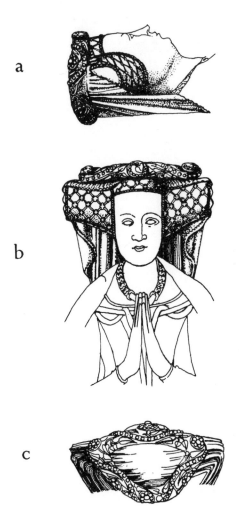

57. 15TH CENTURY, 1ST HALF
(a) Side view of (b). (b) Wide templers and fillets, with pendant veil
behind. (1418) (c) Top view of (b).

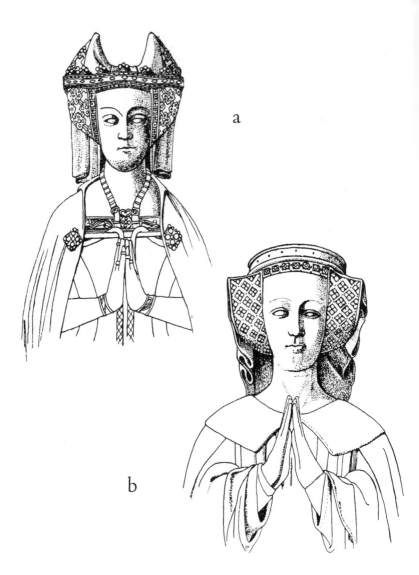

a

b

58. 15TH CENTURY, 1ST HALF
(a) Heart-shaped head-dress draped with veil. (Style of 1420–50.)
(b) Fillet with low templers and veil. Houppelande with flat collar.
(1415.)

part of the forehead, was often attached to a high head-dress. Possibly this device was to counter-balance the backward pull of the top-heavy structure.

(4) *Veils*

(*a*) The *old style* of veil continued to be worn domestically and by the elderly and widows throughout the century [1400–1500].

The *Goffered veil* or 'nebula' head-dress also survived for a time [to 1420].

(*b*) The *Wired veil,* draped over the head behind; the straight edge above the forehead was wired to stand out over the hair, which was generally enclosed in a net and dressed to form bosses above the ears. (Fig. 52c).

Sometimes the border across the forehead was ruched or a small jewelled circlet added. As height increased the wiring over the forehead was bent up at each side to form a deep U, similar to that in example (3) (*a*) [1400–1460].

With *thin gauze veils* and *ruched veils* the wiring might be discarded, the veil being loosely draped.

The *Widow's veil.* The veil and wimple together, at this time indicated widowhood, the veil being made of heavy dark material. The wimple, now called the *barbe,* was stitched in vertical pleats and covered the chin when worn by those of high rank; or was worn below the chin by others. (Fig. 55c).

7. HAIR

This was entirely concealed, except for the following, when the hair was worn long and unconfined:

(*a*) By queens at their coronation.

(*b*) By brides, with wreath or fillet (to the seventeenth century).

(*c*) By unmarried girls, until about 1420, and by children.

(*d*) With the open turban.

Shaved foreheads and temples were in fashion, and eyebrow plucking and face painting continued [1370–1480].

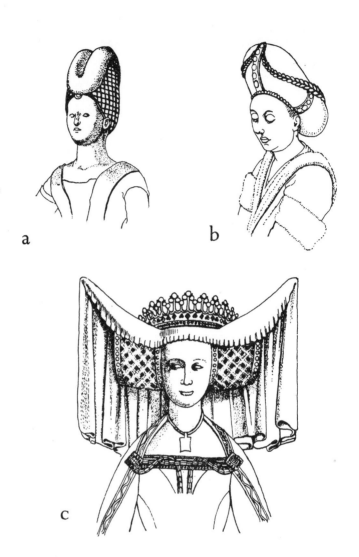

a

b

c

59. 15TH CENTURY, 1ST AND 2ND HALF
HEADWEAR

(a) Circular roll raised to form a U over forehead. Sides covered by hair net. (*c.* 1450–54.) (b) Turban head-dress, the hair brought forward in two plaits fixed to the front instead of hanging loose. (1452.) (c) Horned head-dress with veil wired up over wide templers and sur-mounted by coronet (1416).

8. FOOTWEAR

(1) SHOES followed the men's fashions, but with shorter points during the piked periods. They were often lined. 'Pair of (shoes) of shaved (i.e. polished) leather furred with backs of greys.'

Punceons or *Pinsons* were thin shoes, possibly slippers, but no contemporary description is known. 'Four pairs of punceons of white leather, two furred with pured miniver, two furred with backs of greys.' (1406, Trousseau of Princess Philippa, wife of Eric of Denmark.)

(2) BOOTS were seldom if ever worn.

9. STOCKINGS

Short round hose, gartered above or below the knee.

10. ACCESSORIES

All *Jewellery* as worn by men, including knightly girdles, elaborate necklaces, and SS collars (by Lancastrian ladies of rank).

Also *Pouches,* and occasionally *Daggers.*

Gloves.

Aprons, without bibs, worn domestically.

Elaborate Trimmings, e.g. 'a thousand pearls for embroidering the collar and sleeves of a gown, $16\frac{1}{2}$ oz. of silver-gilt spangs; three tissues of silk' (Princess Philippa's Trousseau, 1406).

Colours: Green and scarlet predominated throughout the period.

Second Half of the Fifteenth Century

MEN

1. THE DOUBLET

Worn over the shirt. Still close-fitting, well padded, waisted and very short, barely covering the hips.

In 1485 it might end at waist level, without a skirt which was optional at this period.

Fastenings. Down the front by lacing, buttons, ties or hooks and eyes. Eyelet holes for trussing the points still used.

Neck

(*a*) With fairly high stand-up collar having a wide V opening in front [1450–1490], becoming wider and deeper, revealing the shirt, over which the collar was joined by lacing [*c.* 1480s].

(*b*) No collar, but a low square-cut neckline [1490–1530], or sloping to a deep V in front, laced across.

Sleeves

(*a*) Close fitting to wrist, and sometimes detachable, being tied on at armholes [1450–1500].

(*b*) Sometimes slashed across at the elbows, the shirt sleeve bulging through; this was occasionally repeated higher up (1480 to 1500, after which slashing increased).

Materials. Velvet and linen common.

'Doublet of red velvet lined with linen cloth.'

'Doublet of white linen cloth.'

'A doublet of crymsyn velvet lined with holand clothe and interlined with busk.' [Wardrobe Accounts of Edward IV, 1481. (B.M. MS. Harl. 4780).]

60. 15TH CENTURY, 2ND HALF

(a) Doublet with detachable sleeves. Long buskins with turn-over tops. Plumed beaver hat (1490-1500). (b) Short doublet laced across stomacher. Shirt showing at neck and through slashed sleeve. Long joined hose. Codpiece. Typical shoes. (1479-87). (c) Jacket (laced across doublet) with hanging sleeves, the doublet sleeves (slashed) emerging. Round cap. Beaver hat slung over shoulder by attached liripipe. Boots. (1479-87). (d) Retainer wearing Earl of Warwick's badge (ragged staff) on his very short jacket. Joined hose. Plumed hat. (1485-90).

'Busk' was also mentioned as an extra lining for the King's satyn doublets. (Ibid.). It was a linen cloth.

2. THE PETTICOAT or WAISTCOAT [1450s–1515]

A short garment, worn for warmth, under the doublet and over the shirt. Usually padded. Tight fitting, with or without tight fitting sleeves. Round neck, usually lower at the back.

'One petticoat of linen cloth stuffed with flock.'

'One petticoat of linen without sleeves' (Sir John Fastolf's Wardrobe Accounts, 1459).

3. THE JACKET (1450 to 1660, but after 1500 usually called Jerkin). Replacing the Cote-hardie. Worn over the doublet, which was always concealed by it at the hem.

Length

(*a*) To mid-thigh, sometimes with side vents.

(*b*) Barely covering the hips, and increasingly uncovering the seat.

Shape. Tight fitting and well waisted, with a narrow belt from which its skirt flared out with some fulness when made in the longer style [1450–1480].

(*a*) Fashionable form, with vertical folds front and back radiating fan-wise up and down from the centre of the waist; the sides smooth and plain.

(*b*) Unfashionable form, plain well-fitting body with full skirt falling in loose folds.

A later style of jacket with formal gathers, longer skirts often made separately from the body and known as '*bases*', was commoner in the sixteenth century [1480–1540. Bases ended *c*. 1540].

'A doublet of blac satyn made and lyned accordingly with a base of a jaket and a stomacher both of blac satyn' [Wardrobe Accounts of Edward IV (1481)].

Mahoitres [1450–1480s] were shoulder pads over which the sleeves were gathered to the shoulder seam. This was a device for producing the characteristic broad shoulders of jackets and gowns.

The Neck

(*a*) No collar, but a round neck with a short wide V opening

136

a   b

61. 15TH CENTURY, 2ND HALF

(a) Jacket with low neck line revealing doublet collar. Loose open
sleeves. Shoes very pointed. Chaperon. (1457.) (b) Fur-trimmed
jacket with hanging sleeve. Doublet sleeve emerging. Small plumed
cap. Piked shoes. (c. 1470–80.)

62. 15TH CENTURY, 2ND HALF

(a) Jacket trimmed with fur. Doublet collar showing above. Pointed
pattens with dark shoes. Chaperon with long liripipe. (c. 1456.) (b) (c)
Jackets with vertically slashed sleeves showing doublet sleeve which in
(c) is also slashed showing shirt sleeve. (c. 1470.)

in front or behind, or a narrow V in front to waist [1450–1480s].

(*b*) A deep V opening in front, the point reaching the waist and revealing the doublet, or a separate chest piece called a 'stomacher', which barely extended below the waist [1480s–1490s].

'Warme your soverayne his petticotte, his doublett and his stomacher . . .' ('Boke of Karvyng', late fifteenth century).

Sleeves

(1) Closed

(*a*) Full above, narrowing to the wrist, without gathers, and there buttoned.

(*b*) Full and gathered into a buttoned wristband. Such sleeves often had a vertical slash generally laced across and revealing the underlying doublet or shirt sleeve.

(2) Open

Full above, tubular, narrowing slightly to the wrist and often rolled back to the elbow, thus producing a short sleeve. The lining gave the appearance of a wide cuff.

(3) Hanging sleeves ('Side sleeves', 'side' or 'syde' meaning 'long').

Open in the form of a wide tube hanging to the knees or lower; often the two were tied together behind to keep them out of the way.

The usual upper slit for the arm was fairly deep.

Materials

Velvet, chamlet, figured satin (the last forbidden to all below rank of knight, by Sumptuary Law of Edward IV), fustian and leather.

Linings of linen or blanket cloth. (Where some of the garment was likely to be hidden by the gown, this might be made of inferior material. See Example (*c*).)

Examples (From Wardrobe Accounts of Sir J. Fastolf, d. 1459).

(*a*) 'Jacket of blue velvet lined in the body with small linen cloth and the sleeves with blanket.'

(*b*) 'Jacket of red velvet, the vents bound with red leather.'

a

b

c

63. 15TH CENTURY, 2ND HALF

(a) Hooded cape. (*c.* 1458–9.) (b) Long gown, shoulders broadened over mahoitres, and low V neck behind. Chaperon. Piked shoes. (*c.* 1460–70.) (c) Long gown, hanging sleeves, one worn normally. Hat with attached liripipe draped over shoulder. (*c.* 1460–70.)

64. 15TH CENTURY, 2ND HALF
(a) Travelling coat and hat (1485-90). (b) Gown, open, fur-trimmed, with hanging sleeves. An early example of the prototype of academic gowns (1497).

(c) 'Jacket, the breast and sleeves of black velvet, the rest of russet fustian.'

(d) 'Jacket of deer's leather, neck edged with black velvet.'

The term COAT at this period was probably a synonym for jacket.

'A clene sherte and breche, a petticote, a doublett, a long cotte, a stomacher, hys socks and hys schone' were the clothes prepared for a man to dress himself in ('Boke of Curtasye'). The term 'coat' may also have applied to a loose overgarment used on journeys, as shown in Fig. 64a. This resembled a pedestrian huke (see p. 106) though with (elbow) sleeves.

4. THE GOWN (Previously called the Houppelande)

As before, but now often, when long, with side or rear vents. Knee-length gowns were called demi-gowns.

The pleats, arranged like massed organ pipes in front and behind for the whole length, were stitched into place at the waist under the belt, the sides being plain.

Fastened all down the front by hooks and eyes or sometimes made double-breasted.

Mahoitres to broaden the shoulders were characteristic.

Neck

(1) The short upright collar with rounded or blunt corners sloping to a V in front continued for a few years [1425–1460].

(2) No collar
    (*a*) Round neck [1425–1500]
    (*b*) With V at the back [1430–1480s]
    (*c*) With U at the back [1450–1470]
    (*d*) With V in front [1430–1465]

(3) A flat square-cut collar at the back, continued forward over the shoulders in long broad revers, sometimes reaching down to the hem in front; often faced with fur [1485–1540].

Belt optional during last quarter of century, the gown being:
    (*a*) Tied at the waist by a narrow girdle of silk ribbon, or
    (*b*) Hanging loosely without a belt, the front left open. Typically ceremonial. Cf. academic gowns of today.

Sleeves

(1) Open. Plain and cylindrical to wrist, or ceremonially, wide at wrist, sometimes rolled up to make a short sleeve. Not very common [1415–1485].

(2) Closed. Usually very full; plain or gathered at the shoulder, and shaped to the wrist without a band, or gathered into a wristband. Any combination of these allowable [1405–1500].

(3) Hanging. Of the open cylindrical type with large upper opening down the front seam, for the arm [1430–1625].

Fur borders continued.

Linings usual, but not invariable.

Materials (from Household Accounts of Sir John Fastolf):—
'Gown of cloth of gold with side sleeves surplice-wise.'

65. 15TH CENTURY, 2ND HALF

Gown with stand-up collar sloping to a V in front. Very full sleeves. Slightly modified 'bowl crop'. (*c.* 1450–60.)

'Gown of blue velvet upon velvet, furred with marten, and purfled (i.e. edged) of the same.'
'One red gown leveret-lined.'
'Gown of cloth of green.'
'One side scarlet gown, not lined.'
Edward IV's Wardrobe Accounts (1481) mention:—
'A demy Gown of Russet lined with clothe.'

5. THE HUKE [1455–1480]

Very rare except for the *pedestrian tabard*. Ground length. The front and back panels were either (*a*) Bound to the waist by a girdle, or

(*b*) The front panel alone was secured by the girdle, the back panel falling loose like a cloak.

Some hukes had sleeves, and were trimmed with fur; some were dagged. 'One jagged huke of black sengle' (Wardrobe Accounts of Sir John Fastolf, 1459).

CEREMONIAL MANTLES continued.

6. CLOAKS

Very rare; used for extra warmth and for travelling.

Capes, thigh length and sometimes hooded, occasionally worn.

7. HOSE

Continued as 'tights', gradually extending higher until the waist was reached (*c.* 1475].

The 'breech' was the name given to the portion covering the seat. This was sometimes of a different colour and even different material from the legs [*c.* 1485]. It was often decorated with small puffs, embroidery, or with a network of crossed bands [*c.* 1490].

Parti-coloured hose returned to fashion in 1485. Striped hose were also popular.

Trussing of hose continued, either to the doublet or to the 'waistcoat'.

The *Codpiece* remained in fashion.

Over-stockings, thick, and loosely fitting, and turned down with a broad fold at the knee, were sometimes worn. The *shape* of the feet as for shoes and boots.

Separate hose still worn by labourers.

8. FOOTWEAR

(1) BOOTS OR BUSKINS. Long, well up the thigh and loose or fitting the leg and laced up on the inner or outer side; far more popular now than during the first half of the century. Used for riding and walking. Deep turned-over tops were common [1450–1500].

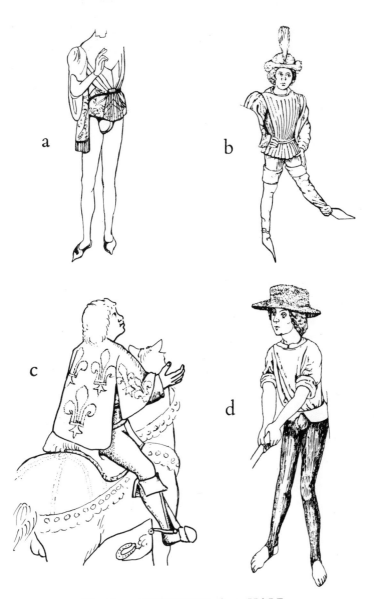

a

b

c

d

66. 15TH CENTURY, 2ND HALF

(a) Jacket with formal gathers, embroidery and hanging sleeves. Slippers. (*c.* 1468). (b) Jacket with formal folds. Long buskins with turn-over tops. Plumed hat. (*c.* 1460). (c) Messenger in tabard over very short jacket and hose. Boots with turn-overs. Spurs with rowels. (1485-90). (d) Peasant's hose with stirrup feet. Summer hat. Codpiece.

145

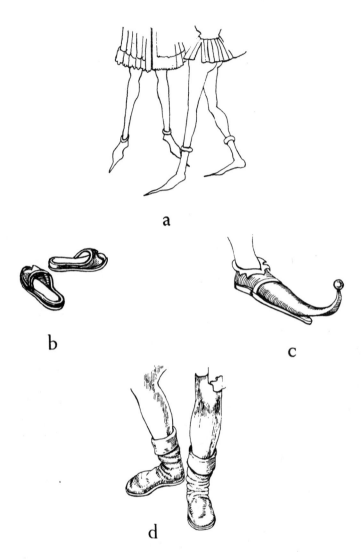

67. 15TH CENTURY, 2ND HALF
FOOTWEAR

(a) Shoes and boots with long points, piked. (1467-68). (b) Late leather pattens. (1498-99.) (c) Piked shoe with wooden patten of very simple design. (d) Short buskins. (1498-99).

Short buskins continued in use.

Shape of foot

(*a*) Short points [1450–1460].

(*b*) Piked [1460–1480].

(*c*) Shorter points [1480–1490].

(*d*) Duck-billed, i.e. square with rounded corners becoming splayed towards 1510 [1490–1515].

(2) SHOES

Some continued with the high cut round the ankle, but most adopted the new style which was characteristic; cut with a deep V on both sides, leaving a long pointed tongue in front of the ankle, and a similar flap behind the ankle. 'Single or double-soled'.

Slippers with open tops occurred, but were uncommon.

(3) PATTENS. These continued, their most fashionable period being from 1440–1460.

(4) SLOPPES [1481]. A kind of shoe mentioned in Wardrobe of Edward IV. Made of blue, red and tawny Spanish leather; some lined with black velvet, others unlined. 'A pair of slops of black leather at 18d a pair' was one of the payments to the king's shoe-maker.

Possibly an overshoe, such as a pantofle (or mule) mentioned in 1496 (Linthicum).

N.B. The name was also applied to a mourning garment shaped like a cassock, e.g. 'A duke, for his gown, slope and mantille, 16 yards at 10s the yard'. (B. M. MS Egerton 2642 f.203v)

9. HEAD WEAR

(1) The HOOD was worn occasionally for a few years, especially on horseback. '1 rydyng hode of rede felwet with iiii jagys' (Wardrobe Accounts of Sir John Fastolf, 1459).

(2) THE CHAPERON continued until *c.* 1470, and longer with the elderly and peasants.

(3) HATS

(*a*) Large crown with flat or rounded top, and broad or narrow brim turned up or down [1450–1480s].

(*b*) Round crown ('bowler' style), the brim rolled or closely turned up or down. Commonly trimmed with upright feather

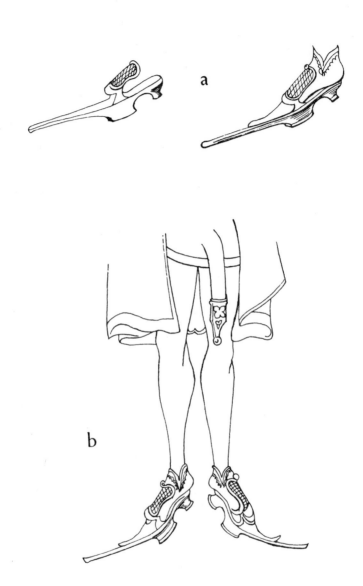

68. 15TH CENTURY, 2ND HALF
(a) Piked patten without and with shoe, showing raised sole and heel.
(b) Pattens worn (1425-40, but style popular in mid-century).

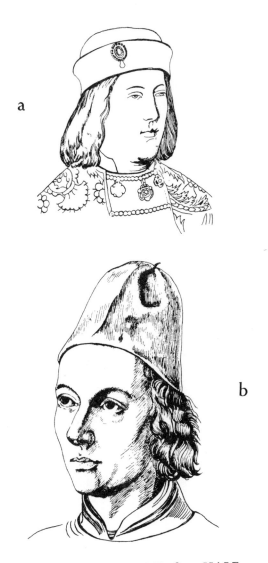

a

b

69. 15TH CENTURY, 2ND HALF

(a) Small round cap, close turned-up brim, and jewelled ornament.
Hair style (p. 150, 10 (c)). (Style 1475-1500.) (b) Turkey bonnet.
(1462).

in front or behind, and attached by jewelled ornament [1400–1500].

(*c*) Tall tapering crown with rolled brim or none [1445–1485].

(*d*) Tall tapering crown with brim peaked in front and turned up behind, a variation of similar styles in previous period and fourteenth century [1430–1460].

(*e*) Large ballooned crown [1430–1460].

(*f*) Plain beaver with moderate crown and brim; attached liripipe for slinging the hat over the shoulder. Frequently carried in this way when another style was being worn [1445–1500].

(*g*) Straw hats of various simple shapes.

(*h*) Large upturned bowl-shaped brim with low crown and large plume of ostrich feathers sometimes spangled. Worn at the back of the head, or slung by strings on the shoulder [1490s–1505].

(4) CAPS known as *bonnets*

(*a*) Felt cap resembling a Turkish fez, varying in height, with and without a stalk, the *Turkey bonnet* [1450-1485].

(*b*) Flat 'pork-pie' cap, close turned up brim and jewelled ornament [1475–1500].

(*c*) A round cap with flat or slightly raised crown and brim closely turned up, but with a gap in front sometimes laced across with gold or silver cords [1480–1515].

10. HAIR (N.B. descriptive terms only)

(*a*) The *Bowl crop* [1410–1460].

(*b*) The *modified bowl crop,* similar, but with the hair longer, partly covering the forehead, ears and back of neck [1450–1475].

(*c*) The '*Page boy*' cut. A forehead fringe, curly or straight; or a centre parting. The rest of the hair hanging down to the neck or sometimes to the shoulders, and frequently waved [1465–1515].

Face generally clean-shaven.

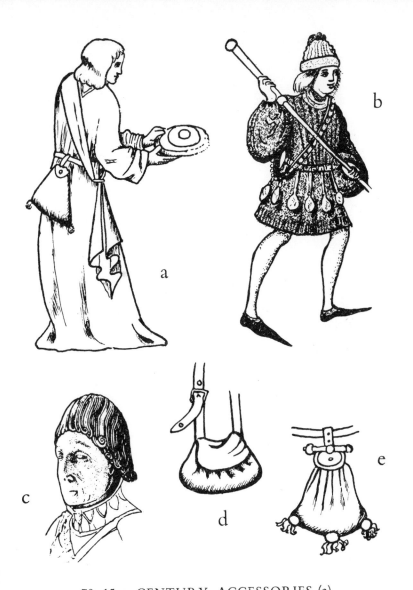

70. 15TH CENTURY, ACCESSORIES (2)

(a) Napkin worn over the shoulder by high ranking servant in long gown. 'Page boy' hair-style. Purse on belt. (1485-90). (b) Folly-bells fastened to gilded waistband and baldrick (shoulder belt). Fine gold chains round neck. Jacket fringed. Cap tasselled. Shoes pointed. Staff. (c. 1500). (c) Modified 'bowl crop' hair-style (1483, a late survival). (d) Shoulder bag worn for travelling. (1485-90). (e) Typical 3-tasselled purse (gypcière) strapped to waistband. (1485-90).

11. ACCESSORIES

As for the first half of the fifteenth century. Heavy *jewelled necklaces* were very prevalent.

Handkerchiefs, called '*Handcoverchiefs*' are mentioned in the Wardrobe Accounts of Edward IV (1481).

A *Breast coverchief* or *stomacher couerchiffe* was worn over the shirt at breast level. Mentioned as being made of holland. (Ibid.)

Muckinder or Mokador (a vulgar term), was a common person's or child's handkerchief or linen square used as a table napkin. 'For eyen and nose, the nedeth a mokadow' (Lydgate's 'Advice to an Old Gentleman who wished for a Young Wife').

Gloves. 'The manufacture must have been adequate for home needs by 1463; in that year King Edward forbade the importation of gloves into England' (Linthicum).

Pouches, sometimes called 'Pokes', corresponding to detachable pockets. '1 russet poke' (Wardrobe Accounts of Sir John Fastolf).

Gypcière, a large 3-tasselled purse, drawn in at the top and strapped to the waistband by a single strap, was now most fashionable. (Fig. 70, a and e).

Baldrick, a jewelled shoulder belt which might be six inches wide, was worn on ceremonial occasions by the nobility (Fig. 50, b).

Follybells. Youths still wore these on waist or shoulder belts.

Jewelled collars, and *chaplets* were still worn. (Fig. 78, a).

Staves or Walking sticks, often about 4 feet long, were used.

Second Half of
the Fifteenth Century

WOMEN

1. THE KIRTLE

Continued in use but was rarely visible. If worn uncovered, this was an act of penance.

2. THE GOWN.

Previously called the *Houppelande*.

Worn over the Kirtle, and now women's principle upper garment. Its styles changed rapidly between 1450 and 1460, the old and new forms overlapping.

NEW STYLE I [1450–1480s]

The formal tubular folds were discarded, and the skirt fell in loose flowing lines from the fairly high waist to a very ample width on the ground. Long trains were common.

(1) *The Bodice*, was at first gathered in at the waist. The V neck was edged with revers as formerly, but at the back the V was not always carried downwards, the collar curving low round the neck.

The Bodice later fitted closely; the revers tended to be placed further off the shoulders, baring the neck, which was cut low in front with a curved or straight edge; the revers being brought down in an open V to the waist, or continued under the belt to a level lower still.

The collar was frequently furred, and always matched the cuffs.

The wide V opening was often laced across the kirtle bodice, or

b

a

c

71. 15TH CENTURY, 2ND HALF
NEW STYLES

(a) Gown style I (p. 153). 'High crowned bonnet' head-dress (p. 161, 5f).
(b) Gown style II (p. 155). Similar head-dress with lower crown. (1490).
(c) Gown style III (p. 157). Turban head-dress. (1479-1488).

occasionally over an ornamental 'fill-in' called a *stomacher*. Only very rarely was the V opening not edged with a collar.

(2) *Sleeves*. Three types:

(*a*) Immense funnel-shapes, with the lower end of the wide aperture falling towards the hem [1450–1460s].

(*b*) Loose fitting and cylindrical to the wrist, usually cuffed or edged with fur [1450–1470s].

(*c*) Tight fitting, ending at the wrist in either a large turned-back cuff or a mitten-like prolongation to the knuckles [1460–1520].

(Both were probably the same cuff turned up or down.)

Mahoitres were not worn by women.

(3) *The Belt*

Usually very broad; often embroidered; worn at a high waist level, well pulled in.

NEW STYLE II [1470s–1500]

The *bodice* moulded the figure to the waist and, more often, to hip level; there the expanding skirt hung in natural folds of full drapery to the ground; long trains were frequent.

Fastened by almost invisible lacing in front, or sometimes behind.

A seam at the waist joining bodice and skirt began to appear, *c*. 1470, in the construction of gowns.

Occasionally this gown ended just below the knee, acting like a surcoat over the kirtle which swept the ground.

The Neck line was very low, the front edge often curving up into a short point at the centre.

A flat falling collar of the 'bertha' type, frequently of fur, and always matching the cuffs, bordered the neck line, widening out over the shoulders; and passing below the upcurved point in the centre front.

Sleeves. Of the type (*c*) previously described.

The Belt was narrow, usually composed of ornamental metal plaques, and worn loosely round the waist, or more often at hip level; usually finished with a long hanging end.

Occasionally absent.

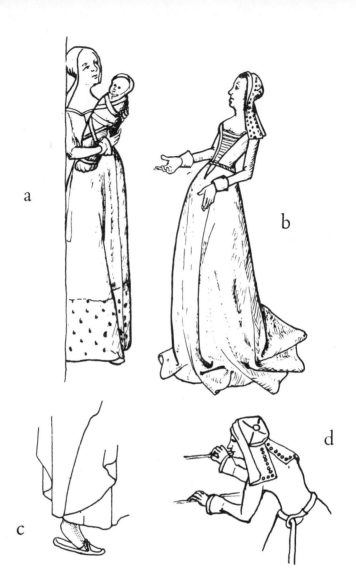

72. 15TH CENTURY, 2ND HALF

(a) Gown with fur at the base. Baby with wrappings and swaddling bands (c. 1485-90). (b) Gown in 'new style I', later type (p. 153). Off-the-shoulder and plunging V neck-line, laced across. Trained skirt. Cuffs turned back. New hood-like head-dress, reflected off face showing contrasting lining (c. 1485-90). (c) Leather patten (1479-87). (d) Back view of a type of hood-like head-dress. Mitten-like cuffs (c. 1485-90).

'My narrow gilt girdle and enamelled girdle of velvet upon satin' (Will of Margaret Odeham of Bury, 1492). '. . . my best corse girdill blewe hernised [adorned] wt. silver and gilt' (Will of Margt. Paston, 1481. *Norfolk Archaeology III*).

In all low-necked gowns, a soft white material in folds, crossing the shoulders to a V front and back, was worn. This was sometimes called a *gorget*, but the Howard ladies (see p. 160) had 'fyne Holande for *nekkercheves*.' Alternatively, large and elaborate necklaces or neck collars were extremely fashionable.

NEW STYLE III

A variation of Style II, and very uncommon in England. The line of the tight-fitting bodice was broken by pleats or gathers stitched down at the centre of the neck edge, front and back, and then allowed to flow free and loose to the ground.

Usually *no belt* was worn.

The *Neck* was moderately low, widening to the shoulders. The *bertha* was shaped in a wide oval, often overlapping the shoulders. When omitted it was replaced by a stitched-down narrow band of material.

The *sleeves* were of the type (2) (*c*) previously described; or, less commonly, *hanging sleeves,* open from above the elbow, the pendant parts forming a broad tippet of ankle length; or tight to the elbow, the kirtle sleeve carried on to the wrist.

NEW STYLE IV [from 1490]

At the close of the century there appeared a loose gown with a square neck, above which might appear the top of the kirtle or the folds of the gorget (or fill-in). This gown was either fastened invisibly down the front, or the bodice was laced across a wide V opening in front, and both styles might be similarly laced behind.

Occasionally the gown hung loose from the shoulders, but usually the bodice was close fitting.

The skirt was always full and trained.

Such gowns could be worn alone, or over the close-fitting kirtle as described. The train was long, and often turned up and fastened to the belt behind, or if no belt was worn it was pinned with a brooch or tied up at this level, or draped over one arm. Thus the lining of rich material was displayed.

a

b

73. 15TH CENTURY, 2ND HALF

(a) Gown style IV (p. 157). Low hood-like head-dress (1495–1500).
(b) Gown style IV with train turned up showing fur lining. Back
lacing to bodice. Low hood with front border turned back and showing
under cap. (c. 1495–1500.)

74. 15TH CENTURY, 2ND HALF
HEADWEAR

(a) (c) Variations of high V-shaped roll with attached ornamental gorget and liripipe. (*c.* 1450-60.) (b) Truncated cone-shaped head-dress with flowing veil. (*c.* 1480.) (d) High crowned bonnet-shaped head-dress with V loop over forehead. (*c.* 1484.)

75. 15TH CENTURY, 2ND HALF

The 'Chimney pot' head-dress with narrow veil looped round chin, known as the Turkey Bonnet. (*c.* 1446).

The *sleeves* were usually large, and very wide at the wrists (this style of gown developed into the characteristic garment of the Tudor period in the next century).

Lining and Trimming of Gowns

The use of fur was still very prevelant.

The wife of Sir John Howard, later Duke of Norfolk, had 'A longe gowne of cremyson velvet furred with menever and pur-felled [edged] wyth ermyn and another gowne of murry clothe furred with martres [marten]' (1465). [Howard Household Book ed. by B. Botfield in *Manners and Expenses of the XIIIth and XVth centuries* (Roxburghe Club, 1841)].

3. THE SIDELESS SURCOAT [1360–1500, and as state apparel up to 1520].

Continued in use, but towards the close of the century it tended to become a ceremonial garment only.

4. MANTLES

These remained unchanged.

'A mantle of white cloth of gold damaske, furred with ermine fastened on her breast with a large lace (cord) curiously wrought with gold and silk with rich knoppes of gold at the end tasselled', was worn by Elizabeth of York, Queen of Henry VII, on the day before her coronation (B.M. Cotton MS. Julius B XII).

5. HEADWEAR

During the second half of the fifteenth century up to 1485–90, all head-dresses were tall, placed high on the head, and worn with a backward tilt.

The hair was shaved up to the lower margin of the tight-fitting headgear, and the ears, with rare exceptions, were left uncovered.

The U loop on the forehead was conspicuous.

Types:

(a) The 'Sausage-shaped' Roll, with deep V over the fore-head, described previously, continued, though it was usually more elongated [1440–1485].

(b) A similar shape with the U over the forehead, but the substructure entirely concealed by a thick veil [1440–1485].

(c) The turban head-dress, increasing in size and height [1440–1485].

(d) The 'chimney-pot' head-dress, so shaped, with a veil attached to the top and allowed to flow behind. Rarely a gorget and liripipe attached instead [1460–1480s].

(e) The 'truncated cone' was the English modification of the French 'hennin' or steeple-shaped head-dress, the latter being avoided in this country. The cone had the shape of an inverted flower-pot, and was draped with a large gauze veil; this flowed down freely behind, and was sometimes so long that it had to be carried over the arm [1460–1480].

(f) The 'High-crowned Bonnet'. In this the crown varied

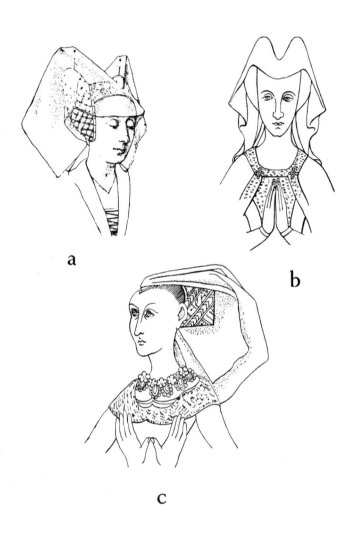

a

b

c

76. 15TH CENTURY, 2ND HALF
HEADWEAR

(a) Butterfly head-dress pinned up over side pieces (rare in England). (1449.) (b) Veil draped in a U over high side pieces. (1458). (c) Butterfly head-dress showing hair strained back into the usual supporting cap. Top of gown style II. Elaborate necklace. (1482.)

a

b

77. 15TH CENTURY, 2ND HALF

(a) Butterfly head-dress of transparent gauze arranged low over forehead. (Style of 1450-85.) (b) Plain linen hood (*c.* 1480's). (Style of 1485-1500). (Both these head-dresses appeared earlier abroad.)

from a short truncated cone to a much lower shape, either flat-topped or sometimes domed. A broad turned-back brim curved round the face and descended stiffly on each side to the shoulders [1460–1490s].

(g) The 'Butterfly Head-dress'. Very characteristic of nearly the whole of the second half of the fifteenth century, surviving all other forms, though infrequent after 1485.

Consisted of a large gauze veil supported on a wire frame, with the usual V dip over the forehead. The whole structure presented the appearance of a pair of diaphanous 'wings' spreading out above the head. It was built up on a small ornamental cap in the shape of a fez, which was worn on the back of the head enclosing all the hair.

Sometimes a transparent fold of gauze was stretched low over the forehead, perhaps to check the head-dress from slipping backwards [1450–1495].

(h) After 1485 and the end of the Yorkist dynasty, a sudden change (coinciding with the new Tudor dynasty) appeared in women's headgear. Only the 'high crowned hood' and the 'butterfly' head-dresses survived, and these not after 1495.

The *new mode* appearing from 1485 (and continuing into the sixteenth century) was a *low hoodlike covering*, worn similarly to the old-fashioned veil, its straight edge framing the face, with the material draped back over the head and falling outwards to the shoulders. This hood was lined with some bright contrasting colour; and the broad fold which was turned back round the face gave a decorative 'surround' and exposed a close-fitting under cap. This was shaped like a coif, and was usually tied under the chin, being made of linen, or velvet often edged with a jewelled embroidery. (From this developed the English 'Gable head-dress').

A *similar hood of plain linen*, with a stiffened edge framing the face, fell in ample folds to the shoulders and neck.

(i) *Fur bonnets.* 'A gentlewoman borne [only she] shall weare an Ermyne or Letise bonnet . . . and, if she be of honourable stoke, to haue two powderings, one before another in the toppe.' B.M. MS Harl. 1776 (c.1493). The "powdering" would be a trimming, e.g. of black lambskin.

78. 15TH CENTURY, 2ND HALF
HEAD-DRESSES. CHILDREN'S DRESS

(a) Henry VI aged 9 months. Typical baby's dress, long to the feet, long sleeves, unadorned. Coroneted 'cap of estate' turned up with ermine. Earl of Warwick wears chaplet and rich collar. (1485-90).
(b) Gown style IV. Black 'hood', turned back with gold. Cap beneath. (1495-1500). (c) Beck worn by young girl with flowing hair (1520 Style from 1495.) (d) Simple caul (c. 1495).

6. INDOOR HEADWEAR

The Fret was an ornamental hair net edged with a jewelled turban-like roll.

The Caul was a close-fitting coif-like head-dress covering the ears; reticulated in gold thread decorated with jewels or pearls, and sometimes lined with taffeta or tissue. When worn with a fillet or coronet it was very like styles at the end of the fourteenth century.

The Beck was a beak-like piece of material worn point forwards above the centre of the forehead; by young girls it was pinned to the hair, by married women fastened under the head-dress. The fashion was not very popular or approved of by authority. Thus, in the 'Order for wearing Apparelle at the time of mourning' it was directed in 1493, 'that in no manner of wise the Beakes be used, for the deformity of the same.' (B.M. MS. Harl. 1776.)

Frontlets were forehead bands worn across the forehead usually with a veil and made of cloth, silk, velvet or gold (Privy Purse Expenses of Elizabeth of York).

7. MOURNING APPAREL

The *Hood*, of the old-fashioned type, but with modifications, was worn for mourning.

Thus in the above-mentioned Order—'A Duchess to weare a plaine hood without clokes[1]', and tippettes (i.e. liripipe) at the hoode, in length to the grounde and in bredth a nayle and half an Inche. Lords daughters and Knightes wifes to wear there hoodes with cloakes; and tippettes in bredth three quarters of a nayle, and in length a yarde Demy, to be pynned upon their Arme.

'The Queenes gentlewomen to weare hoodes with clokes, the tippettes a yarde longe and a ynch brode, to be pynned on the sides of there hoodes. All Chamberers shall weare hoodes with clokes and noe manner of tippetts. Great estates wearing mantelles, when they ride, to have short clokes and hoodes, with narrowe tippetts, to be bounde about there heades; and as soon as they come to court they [are] to lay away there hoodes; and that after the

---

[1] ? shoulder-cape (gorget) of hood.

79. 15TH CENTURY, 2ND HALF
Elaborate jewelled caul worn with coronet. (1498-99.)

first month none to weare hoodes in there betters presence, but when they labour.'

'*Slope* is a mourning Cassake for Ladies and gentlewomen, not open before . . . The Queenes gentlewomen to weare sloppes or Cotharders [cote-hardies].

A *Surcott* is a mourning garment made like a close-bodyed gowne or a straight-bodied gowne [which] is worn under the mantell. The same, for a Countes[s] must have a trayne before and another behinde.' [Ibid.]

8. HAIR

This was completely concealed, or occasionally seen strained back from the forehead when the head-dress was worn very far back and shaving was incomplete.

Face-painting and eyebrow plucking continued in fashion. (To *c.* 1480.)

9. STOCKINGS or Hose as in the first half of the century.

The purchase of "a hose-clothe" for one of Sir John Howard's daughters is recorded in 1465[1].

The hose of the poorer classes were still made of coarse wool.

> She hobles as a gose
> With her blanket hose.
>
> (John Skelton, *Elynour Rummyng, c.* 1490-1500.)

10. FOOTWEAR

SHOES as for men, but never piked.

BUSKINS worn for travelling; e.g. 'For two pair of buskins for the Queen's Grace at her departing into Wales' (Privy Purse Expenses of Elizabeth of York).

PATTENS had short pointed toes with cross straps over the instep, placed well forward; no heel support. These were often worn directly over the hose.

11. ACCESSORIES

As in the first half of the century.

Belts and *Girdles* were very elaborate.

'A little girdle of cloth of gold; another of green damask' and 'A little girdle of silk and gold called a damasent' were given by Sir John Howard to his wife in 1465[2]. The demiceint had front half of goldsmith's work, back half plain silk.

---

[1] and [2] Howard Household Book, Ed. by B. Botfield in *Manners and Expenses of the XIIIth and XV Centuries* (Roxburghe Club, 1841).

Children's Costume in the Middle Ages

BABIES

> *"When the child is born*
> *He must be swaddled."*

> The Treatise of Walter of Biblesworth
> (Early 14th century. Translated from the French)

In mediaeval times babies were always swaddled for the first few months (p. 73, Fig. 29d and p. 156, Fig. 72a).

Swaddling involved wrapping up the baby's body, the arms and legs enclosed, and then bandaging round this from neck to feet. This, it was thought, would save the limbs from damage by careless handling, and there was also a mediaeval belief that limbs left free in infancy might show deformity later on.

Christening robes for aristocratic or Royal babies were usually very grand. These might consist of a long velvet mantle trimmed with fur and a long silk kerchief extending from the child's head to the feet of the person carrying the infant.

It is uncertain for how long the baby was kept in swaddling clothes, but mediaeval miniatures are known in which quite small babies have the legs loosely draped and the body bare from the waist up. Fig. 78a shows Henry VI at the age of 9 months, wearing a proper dress with long sleeves though of very simple design. An effigy in Scarcliff Church, Derbyshire, portrays a mother with an infant boy, apparently 1½-2 years old, in a similar dress but girdled. He wears a fine neckerchief wrapped round the throat, but is barefooted and bare-headed, with short hair.

NURSERY CHILDREN

For several years after babyhood boys were probably dressed much like girls, as was generally true until the mid-nineteenth century. The accounts kept (in Latin) for Prince Henry in 1273-4 tell a good deal about mediaeval childhood[1]. The household centred on Henry himself, aged 5-6, his little sister Eleanore, 9-10, and his cousin John, 7-8. All three were supplied with the same articles of clothing and had their *robae* made with the same fur-trimmings or silk laces, buttons, etc. (nearly 2 gross of buttons, some gilt, were bought in all). All three received *caligae* (hose) of black *"burnett de worthested"* (specially tectured for a downy surface), linen shifts or smocks (no mention of braies for the boys), shoes, peacock-feathered caps, plain or squirrel-trimmed gloves and a pair with the royal R embroidered on the thumb. Practically everything was ordered in triplicate, the three children being named each time. Almost the only distinction was that coloured silks "for making *laqueos* (laces?), were bought for Eleanore alone, and *"agulets"* were separately ordered for her shoes.

M. A. E. Green[2] gives evidence that the term *roba* meant a triple outfit — kirtle, over-garment and mantle. This would explain why no other main garments were necessary for the children. Two wards of the King, in the same household, boys of 15 and 16, were dressed quite separately and for them tabards of bluet were ordered and also coifs like the men's. They were dressed as adults. Indeed, once past the nursery stage all children, throughout the Middle Ages, were dressed much like their parents. There were, however, some modifications worth noticing.

BOYS

Younger boys' tunics were generally shorter than men's, belts were optional and the head and feet were much more often bare.

[1] Hilda Johnstone. *The Wardrobe and Household of Henry, Son of Edward I.*
Manchester Univ. Press, 1923.

[2] Mary A. E. (Wood) Green. *Lives of the Princesses of England ii.* (Colburn. 1849).

(Fig. 29e, p. 73). In the 15th century their gowns were loose, not full length and often worn without a belt.

In the household of Sir John Howard[1] 'lytelle master Edmond' or 'lytell Edmond' was probably a page, about 10 years old or in his early teens. He was provided, in 1467, with the usual outfit of shirt, doublet, boots, bonnet, two 'semed gownes' etc., but unlike the men of the household he had a 'hode' made for him.

Older boys were dressed exactly like their fathers (Fig. 40b, p. 96). They could be particular, in the 15th century, as to the colour and fit of their best hose, no doubt in order to display a pair of shapely legs. A letter from John Paston (aet. 15) to his mother, 14th September, 1465, 'beseeches' her for;

> 'two pair of hose, one pair black and another pair of russet which be ready made for me at the hosier's . . .'

His brother, William, when a boy at Eton in 1478 was asking for:

> 'A hose cloth, one for holy days of some colour, and another for the working days (how coarse soever it be it maketh no matter) and a stomacher and two shirts and a pair of slippers.'[2]

Correct behaviour for children in relation to their clothes was very carefully ordered. While adults wore headgear even at table, a boy was told:

> 'In halle, in bowre or at the borde
> Hoode or Kappe thou off tho [then]'

Again when 'Speaking with his lord'

> 'Hold of [f] thy cappe and thy hood also
> Tylle thou be byden hit on to do.'
>
> (*Urbanitatis* B.M. MS Cot. Calig. A.II,f. 88) (*c.* 1460)

GIRLS

Little girls were dressed like their mothers, though usually with a simpler design. Even when very small they had skirts down to their feet. Where they differed was about the head, as, unlike

---

[1] *Manners and Expenses in the XIIIth and XVth Centuries* Ed. by B. Botfield (Roxburghe Club, 1841).
[2] *Paston Letters* ed. by A. Ramsay-Knight 1840.

their mothers, they often went bare-headed or a simple veil was worn instead of an elaborate head-dress. (Fig. 17d).

Girls of a marriageable age always let their hair hang loose down to the waist or lower. (Fig. 18b, p. 54, Fig. 78c, p. 165).

ACCESSORIES

In the 15th century, apparently, even little boys wore the popular purse or pouch. Some more rhyming rules (1430) had to forbid its use as a cache for titbits from the table.

Handkerchiefs by now were coming into vogue for the upper classes and Hugh Rhodes (in the early 16th century) instructs as follows:

'Blow not your nose on the napkin
Where you should wype your hande;
But cleanse it in your handkercher.'
(*Book of Nurture* in *Babees Book* ed. by E. Rickert 1923)

Working People's Costume in the Middle Ages

Recent research has thrown further light on what was worn by men and women at work, a subject less documented than the costume of leisured and well-to-do people. In the following notes this new work is collated with the various references to peasant dress that have been made in the foregoing chapters, so as to give an overall picture.

Until the 15th century there was little distinction between the classes as regards the main components of their costume, but there were always important differences in the materials used and often minor but consistent differences of detail.

MATERIALS

Largely homespun and never of silk (too dear) nor cotton (not yet introduced). Upper garments were made of;

(*a*) coarse wool, such as *frieze, kersey, kendal,* or the type (from 15th c.) called *russet;* also *cauri-mauri* and *stamin.*

(*b*) *Fustian,* a twilled velveteen-like mixture of wool and linen.

(*c*) coarse linen or sackcloth. ·

That this was normal wear for the rustic is shown by the fact that Ceres, in *Assembly of the Gods* (1420) denotes her patronage of the landworker by appearing in a 'garment of sak cloth'. But in times of prosperity:–

> 'the poor and small folk . . . bedeck themselves in fine colours and fine attire whereas (were it not for their pride and their conspiracies) they would be clad in sackcloth as of old.'
>
> John Gower *Speculum Meditantis* (1375)
> Trans. G. G. Coulton. 1938.

(d) Leather, for jackets and footwear.

For underwear there was coarse linen.

For winter cloaks, capes and the gorgets of hoods there was sheepskin with the wool outside (p. 59 Fig. 21 f; p. 61, fig. 22a) or the fur of rabbit, squirrel, etc.

COLOURS

'Hodden grey' i.e. neither bleached nor dyed; russet brown; green, especially in kendal. The dyes in use were very limited until the 14th century. One of the commonest, and the only blue, was indigo from home cultivated woad. But by c.1490 a very shabby old woman might wear a "Kyrtel of Brystow red" for best (Skelton). Cloth hoods, cloaks and even cotes were surprisingly often lined and a contrasting material would be used if possible.

MEN

LANDWORKERS — 9th to 12th CENTURIES

Tunic or 'kirtle' and supertunic were rather short, at least on young men (p. 23, Fig. 5b shows 'Joseph's coat' held by one of his shepherd brothers). Typically the tunic would be hitched up on one side or both by a belt, or by the braies girdle beneath. The supertunic was comparatively rare, the *cloak* taking its place if overgarment was needed. This was generally hip-length and shoulder-fastened and was often used for carrying grain, stones, etc.

In the 12th century a closed *hooded cape* of sheepskin was popular, especially with shepherds (p. 29, Fig. 7b).

For underwear in the 10th and 11th centuries there might be only a loin cloth under a shirt. Later *braies* were usual; workers of the 12th century favoured long braies like trousers but slit at the ankle, which, worn without any covering, gave workmen a very distinctive appearance (Fig. 80b). For work in summer nothing was worn but braies, with or without a shirt and hat.

80. WORKING PEOPLES' DRESS

(a) 11th c. labourer. Short tunic hitched up by belt. Bare legs and head. (b) Labourer (*c.* 1155). Long braies slit at ankle. Shirt. Shady hat. (c) Monumental mason (a master craftsman?) 1433. See p. 178. (d) Blacksmith's wife in apron (*c.* 1330). (e) Poor man's footless hose, pulled up over braies. Tied garters (*c.* 1280). (f) Smith's apron-fronted boot (*c.* 1360). (g) Porter, 1433. Doublet long-skirted, with vent. Loose separate hose. (h) Stevedore, 1433. Tunic-like garment.

M

Leg and footwear.

(*a*) Feet very often bare (Fig. 80a & b).

(*b*) Footless hose (p. 30, Fig. 8a).

(*c*) Leg bandages with or without soled hose beneath, much used by those exposed to cold etc., and favoured to this day by shepherds in some parts of the country.

(*d*) Ill-fitting cloth hose either soled or, for example in stubble fields, worn with boots.

Headwear. Caps, wide brimmed hats, improvised fillets of straw.

LANDWORKERS — 13th and 14th CENTURIES

Cote (formerly tunic) still loose and belted at waist, in contrast to typical gipons (p. 46, Fig. 14d, a boatman; p. 59, Figs. 21e-g; p. 67, Figs. 26 compare b and c with a).

Surcote, if worn, usually sleeveless, or of garnache shape almost like a smock (the 'tabard' of Chaucer's plowman).

Courtepy or short cloak for winter.

Braies, usually short (p. 59, Fig. 21e), sometimes calf-length. For hot work, braies and shirt only.

Leg and footwear.

(*a*) Footless hose (Fig. 80c), sometimes fringed at the ankle and worn with the feet bare.

(*b*) Stirrup-hose (p. 61, Fig. 22a).

(*c*) Hose long or rolled at the knee, still often soled but also worn with strap shoes (p. 81, Fig. 33a and b). Langland's plowman wore much mended 'knoppede shon,' presumably hob-nailed shoes.

(*d*) Boots.

(*e*) Piked shoes, for the better off, when in vogue.

The *hood*, with or without gorget, was universally used for warmth (p. 67, Figs. 26b and c).

Hats were often worn with the persistent *coif* and sometimes with a hood as well (p. 46, Fig. 14d; also p. 58 Fig. 20c).

Cloth mitts were very popular (p. 67, Figs. 26b, c and d).

Waist belts with attached purses were worn even in the fields. A shepherd's belt carried a knife, a tarbox and other medicaments (Fig. 26c), and often a musical pipe. Messengers' belts carried a wallet for letters.

LANDWORKERS — 15th CENTURY

Less extreme shortness and tightness of garments than was in vogue. Shepherds still wore 13th century clothes.

> 'In russet clothing tyret hym tho [then]
>   In kyrtil [tunic] and in curstbye [cape]
> And a blak furred hode.'
>   *Tale of King Edward and the Shepherd*
>   (15th Century.)

The usual wear for any labourer is that shown on the stevedore in Fig. 8oh — a loose, belted garment like the tunic of earlier centuries. Instead of tight-fitting hose he still often wore loose stockings of coarse cloth, as in Fig. 8og, and instead of shapely shoes, loose boots.

Men generally worked in their kirtles, cotes or doublets, without any overgarment. This, if worn at all, was usually a knee-length sleeveless huke or a gown without exaggerated sleeve styles. Men harvesting are often seen in only a short shirt and joined hose (presumably soled). The old-fashioned courtepy persisted.

Foot and legwear.

(*a*) For peasants' 'separate hose' and 'leggings' see pp. 107, 108 and 111.

(*b*) Stirrup-hose, worn by a man thrashing, are shown on p. 145 (Fig. 66d). Other styles as before.

Hoods long outlived the fashion.

Hats — typically wide brimmed felts and straws — changed less than with the upper classes, and since hoods were still worn as such, the chaperon was rarer.

OTHER WORKERS IN GENERAL

Craftsmen and tradesmen, especially town-dwellers, naturally tended to be more fashionable in dress than other workers. The masons in Fig. 49c (p. 116) and Fig. 80c wear doublets well-fitting above the waist, in contrast to the stevedore's tunic (Fig. 80h); both have fashionable hose. Smartness, however, was restrained, not only for financial reasons but also because of Sumptuary Laws. In Henry IV's reign it was decreed that no man of low estate should wear:-

'large hanging sleeves open or closed, nor his gown
so long as to touch the ground'

and

'That no yeoman shall wear any other furs than those of
foxes, of conies and of otters.'

The hierarchy — apprentice, serving-man or journeyman, and master craftsman — was expressed in costume, e.g. apprentices wore no headgear in their master's presence and the latter wore more important-looking hats than their employees. (The Master Mason's black hat of today's Freemasonry is a survival of this distinction). Compare with one another the two masons mentioned above. The balloon-hatted example (Fig. 80c) is probably a master craftsman.

Livery colours were sometimes worn by the workmen of large employers of labour. For example builders working for the Crown were sometimes compelled to wear red liveries in an attempt to prevent their escape into more lucrative employment.

From the 14th century onwards most London crafts and tradesmen had their Guild or Company, with its ceremonial livery for the higher ranks, i.e. a distinctively coloured hood and surcote (later gown). The latter was often parti-coloured and trimmed with 'budge'. The style of ceremonial Company Liveries today is a clear survival of 15th century costume.

Only a few garments appropriate for special types of work developed in the Middle Ages.

Leather aprons. 'Smoky smiths . . . of a bull's hide are their big aprons.' [B. M. MS. Arundel 292, (c. 1350)]. Smiths, tanners,

178

sometimes masons (Fig. 80c) had leather aprons. The bib, if any, was either shoulder-strapped (Fig. 80d) or triangular and brooched.

Cloth aprons, probably of unbleached wool or sackcloth, were generally used by butchers, sometimes by masons, but little, if at all, by bakers, menservants and landworkers, until the 16th century.

Special footwear. An ankle-boot, with an apron-front covering the fastening as a protection from molten metal, appears to have been used in the 14th century by smiths (Fig. 80f). This was remarkably like the metal-moulder's clog of today. On horseback most men wore only ordinary soled hose or shoes, not boots.

In the absence of waterproof clothing of any kind, well-diggers for example wore nothing at all but a short shirt. Seamen worked, at times, stripped to the braies or stark naked.

MEN DOMESTIC SERVANTS IN LARGE HOUSEHOLDS

(a) *Uppermost ranks*, e.g. marshall, page, and all who valeted or otherwise personally served their master. These were themselves nobles or gentry and dressed as such. In costume, the man shown in Fig. 19b (p. 56) differs only from the master he is dressing by wearing no ornament or headgear. A man waiting at table was always bare-headed and even in the 11th century conventionally wore a long, often fringed, scarf-like napkin round the neck or over the shoulder (p. 67, Fig. 26e and f; p. 151, Fig. 70a). The ends of this often served the purpose of white gloves when he held a dish etc., as in Fig. 26f. Instructions for a Panter or Butler are given by John Russell in his *Book of Nurture*, c. 1460, (in *Babee's Book*, ed. by E. Rickert, 1923.)

'Put a towel round your neck, for that is courtesy . . .
. . . Take the end of the towel in your left hand . . .
together with the salt cellar and . . . the other end
in your right hand with the spoons.'

In the 15th century the rank among those serving was marked by the length of their gowns. The man in Fig. 70a would be the most eminent of the servers.

(b) *Liveried Servants* had their clothes provided, in their master's family colours, and from the 15th century had his badge embroidered on their outer garments (p. 135, Fig. 60d). True tabards appear to have persisted, with heralds and messengers, for the express purpose of this display (p. 145, Fig. 66c). Domestic servants were notorious for their love of fashion. In 1411, when streaming tippets were in vogue, Occleve says that the streets were positively swept by the 'long sleeves of impecunious grooms.'

(c) *Menial ranks.* Among male servants, the cooks and carvers, but apparently only they, wore aprons. A primitive form of this, in *c.*1340, is shown on p. 66 (Fig. 25d).

WOMEN

Working women followed the prevailing mode in the general cut of their clothes, always wearing long skirts and sometimes trains. The main points of difference, apart from materials, are as follows:

(a) Skirts were sometimes tucked up by the belt, as in Fig. 54b (p. 124). Only the very poor, like the labourer's wife in the *Creed of Piers Plowman*, had them 'cut very high' to save material, but in the 15th century they were often short enough to show the ankles.

(b) From the 14th century onwards, a bib-less *apron* was worn for cooking, milking, working in the fields, even spinning. Probably of coarse linen, it was frequently embroidered. (p. 70, Fig. 27a and d).

(c) The *supertunic* or *surcote* was less often worn than by the upper classes. In the Lambeth Bible (12th century) it is depicted on Ruth, who is gleaning, with its very wide sleeves knotted behind her head, out of the way. It was something of an encumbrance.

(d) For extra warmth, *cloaks*, perhaps easier to make, were often preferred to supertunics. In the 9th to 12th centuries these were usually closed and of thigh-length; thereafter they were open, and a shepherdess might wear one reaching the ground. She sometimes drew it over her head, as does the upper class woman of an earlier date in Fig. 10d, (p. 37).

(e) *Moderation in fashion.* As with the men, Sumptuary Laws had a restraining influence.

'First none shall weare an Ermine or Letise bonnet unless she be a gentlewoman borne hauinge Armes'
BM. MS. Harl. 1776. (1481).

For comfort, kirtles worn actually at work were comparatively loose bodiced even in mid-fifteenth century and had loose sleeves with no extremes of shape.

Head-dresses too were much less varied and elaborate than with ladies. The simple veil and the hood retained their popularity throughout. Both are worn by the woman using weeding crotch and hook shown on p. 73 (Fig. 29b). Again, in Fig. 54b (p. 124) the village woman, dating as late as 1433 wears a typical old-style hood outdoors. The head-dress of the ale-wife in Fig. 54c (incomplete in the original) appears to be a short veil with side lappets tied together on the crown of the head.

Both women are unfashionable in being seen in their kirtles, wearing no gown.

The ale-wife lacks all adornment and has a skirt made to clear the feet. Altogether in her appearance, sharply contrasting with her wealthier contemporaries, she might represent the elderly working woman in almost any period of time.

Glossary

OF MATERIALS, COLOURS, AND TERMS OF MULTIPLE OR UNCERTAIN MEANING NOT DEFINED IN THE TEXT

(*N.B.*—The mediaeval spelling was, of course, very variable, the same word often appearing in different forms.)

AGLET, AIGULET or AIGLET. The metal tag to a lace (called a point).

AULMONIERE or ALNER. A purse.

BALANDRANA. A wide cloak for travellers, twelfth and thirteenth centuries.

BARME CLOTH. Apron (Chaucer).

BASELARD. A long dagger worn by civilians (see John Torell's Will) [1400].

BAUDEKIN. Silk cloth with warp of gold thread.

BESSHE. The skin of a doe (?) 'A gown furred with Besshe' [1422].

BETEN. Embroidered with fancy subjects.

BEVER. Beaver.

BICE. Skin of female deer.

BIRRUS or BUREL. A thick rough woollen cloth.

BISS or BISSYN. Fine linen.

BLIAUT, BLIAUD, BLIAUS. A term chiefly of 11th and 12th c. In France, (*a*) A costly material. (*b*) A man's garment worn with armour. (*c*) A man's or woman's court dress [Goddard]. A man's or woman's over-tunic [Evans].

BOTEWS, BOTUYS. Correspond to buskins 'Pair Botews of spanyssh leder above the Knee . . . paire botews sengle blac leder unto the knee' (Wardrobe Accounts of Edward IV) [1481].

BRANCHED VELVET. Figured velvet.

BROCHED CLOTH. Cloth worked with words or ornaments of gold upon it.

BROELLA. A coarse cloth.

BROWNE SWYKE. A kind of linen cloth probably made at Brunswick.

BRUSSEL CLOTH. A linen.

BUDGE or BOGEY. Lambskin with the wool dressed outwards.

BURNET. A cloth of brown colour. Thirteenth century.

BURRELL. Cloth used by working class. Thirteenth century.

BYSSINE. A fine cotton or flax material. Thirteenth century.

CADACE. Flock for padding garments.

CADDIS or CRUEL. A worsted mixed with wool.

CAMELINE. An imported cashmere.

CAURI-MAURI or CARY. A coarse rough textile.

CAMLET or CHAMLETT. A stuff of wool and goat's hair.

CAPA PLUVIALIS or CHAPE À PLUIE. A large cloak to protect against rain.

CAMISIA. Shirt or smock.

CAMOCA. A rich silk fabric, rare in England.

CANVAS. A textile of hemp or of coarse linen.

CELESTINE. A light blue form of Plunket.

CENDAL. A silk textile resembling a coarse Sarcenet.

CHAINSE. French term for long tunic. Eleventh to Thirteenth century.

CHAISEL. A fine linen for smocks.

CHALON. A cloth or garment napped on both sides (Chaucer).

CHAMMER. A jacket with chequered open-work pattern.

CHAMPEYN. A fine linen cloth. Fifteenth century.

CHEKLATON. A costly silk embroidered in chequered knots.

CHELE. Fur from the marten's throat.

CIRCLET. A metal fillet worn by ranks below the nobility.

CLOT SHOEN. Shoes shod with thin iron plates.

COAT or COTE. The term 'cote' occurs in French literature as early as 1159 (Goddard), and by the thirteenth century was common both in England and on the Continent, apparently replacing the tunic. It represents a simple type of everyday dress worn by both sexes and all classes. The word was rarely used for women's attire after the 1420s, and even previously gown or kirtle was more usual. Not until the sixteenth century did cote or coat begin to take on the modern meaning of an outer garment.

COCKERS. High laced boots worn by countrymen ('Piers Plowman').

COGWARE. A coarse common cloth resembling frieze.

COTTON. (The term as used in mediaeval England). Woollen imitation of Continental cotton cloths. "To Cotton" = to give a downy surface.

COUCHED. Trimmed (Chaucer).

COURTEPY or CURSTBYE. A short cloak of coarse cloth.

CRACOWES. Long-toed boots or shoes. [c. 1360s].

CREMYLL. 'Cotton' openwork or lace. Fourteenth century.

CUT WORK. In the fourteenth and fifteenth centuries signified the cutting of the borders of garments into fanciful shapes, i.e. 'dagging'. In the sixteenth century it was a special kind of lace.

CYCLAS. A rich stuff of purple colour, imported.

DEMYSENT. A half girdle. Only front half ornamental. Fifteenth century.

DORELET. A hairnet embroidered with jewels.

ENBRAUDE. Embroidered.

ENBRAUDEN. Embroider.

ENGREYNEN. To dye in grain (dyed in the thread before weaving).

FALDING. A coarse cloth resembling Frieze (Chaucer).

FALWE. Yellow.

FERRET-SILKE. Coarse silk.

FLEMYSSHE CLOTH. A linen.

FLURT-SILKE. Figured silk.

FOYNES. Skin of Polecat.

FRIEZE. A napped rough cloth.

FRONTLET. A forehead band of cloth, silk, or velvet. Fifteenth century.

FROUNCE. The modern flounce. Fourteenth century.

FUNES or FOYNES. Marten skins.

FUSTIAN. A coarse twilled cloth of 'cottoned' wool and linen combined.

FYCHEUX. Fur of the Foumart, 'otherwise called the Polecat or Fichet' [1418].

GAZZATUM. A fine silk or linen gauze. Thirteenth century.

GENETS. See Ionetis.

GIPCIÈRE or GYPCIÈRE or GIPSER. A pouch or purse.

GIRDELSTEDE. The waist (Saxon).

GITE. A gown (Chaucer).

GRISE. A grey fur of Russian squirrel.

HANSELINE or HAUSELINE. Not identified, but probably a jacket. 'Cutted slops or hanselines' condemned by the Parson in Chaucer's 'Canterbury Tales' were garments made too short for decency.

HATERE. Attire.

HERYGOUD. A type of Garde-Corps [Boucher] (13th and early 14th centuries).

HOLLAND CLOTH. A linen cloth.

HOWVE. A hood (Chaucer). Or cap (Saxon).

HURE. A cap. Thirteenth and fourteenth centuries.

INDE. Azure-coloured.

IONETIS. The genet, the fur of which resembles the marten's.

JORNADE. A kind of cloak.

KENDAL. A coarse green cloth.

KENNEL. The triangular head-dress for women, end of fifteenth century.

KERSCHE. Kerchief.

KERSEY. A double-twilled Say.

KIRTLE. Of Saxon origin, and most commonly used as given in the text. But it was a 'term which has been applied, at different periods, to nearly every imaginable garment worn by male or female in these islands—a petticoat, safeguard . . . long mantle . . . an apron, a jacket and a loose gown' (Planché 'Cyclopaedia of Costume') . .

KNOP. A button or a hob-nail (Piers Plowman). Also a tassel.

KOURTE-BY. See Courtepy.

LACE. Before the sixteenth century signified a small cord or tie, e.g. shoe lace. 'Drew a lace of silk full clere; adowne then fell his mantyll' (B.M. MS. Harl. 2252).

LACH. Cloak or mantle (Saxon).

LAKE. A fine lawn (Chaucer).

LETTICE. A fur resembling Ermine.

LIBBARD. Leopard. Green gown furred with libbards. (Will of John Ryngfeld, 1439).

MARTRONS, MARTRES. Martens. 'The most beautiful of all the Weasel kind'.

MUSTERDEVILLIS. 'A kind of mixed grey woollen cloth' (Halliwell). Etymology uncertain. Probably a cloth woven at Montivilliers, Normandy.

NIFLES. A sort of veil. Fifteenth century.

NOUCH or OUCH. A jewelled clasp or buckle (Chaucer).

PALTOCK. Some kind of a jacket or gipon, of Spanish origin, and introduced into England during the reign of Edward III.

PAMPILION. A fur.

PELLARD. A garment resembling a super-tunic.

PEPLUS. A large coverchief or veil, twelfth century. Later a very large shawl-like mantle used by men.

PELURIN. Purfled or edged with fur.

PERSE. A bluish grey. Also a material.

PILION. A round hat (Piers Plowman).

PILCHE. A coat or cloak of skins or fur. In Henry V's wardrobe after his death there were two pilches of 'crist-gray' fur.

PLUNKET. A coloured cloth, originally of fine quality.

POINTS. Ties for attaching hose, as described in the text. They were originally the metal tags on thongs of leather, but the term was transferred to the thongs when the tags were called by the French name aiguilette—anglicised to Aglet.

PONGE. A purse (Chaucer).

PONYET. A cuff of a sleeve, fifteenth century.

POPLE. Fur from the back of a squirrel, fifteenth century.

POULAINES. Long-pointed shoes or boots.

POUNSONED. Punched with a bodkin.

POWDERED. Sprinkled over, e.g. A pair of vestments of white damask, powdered with bears and ragged staves of gold.' (Will of Elizabeth Lady Latimer, 1480). Decoration on leather. Dots of fur trimmings.

PRANKEN. To arrange the folds of a gown.

PUKE. The colour puce; also a stuff commonly used for making hose and gowns.

PURFLE. A border of trimming.

RAISED GOWN. One with a new nap set on the material.

RAY. A striped cloth, fourteenth century.

RAYNES. A fine linen, originally from Rennes.

RENO. A short mantle of precious furs, possibly hooded (Norman).

ROKETTE, ROCKET. A woman's loose upper garment.

ROSKYN. Fur of the squirrel in summer.

RULLIONS. A rough kind of shoe, fifteenth century.

RUSSET. A dark brown colour; also a coarse cloth.

SAMITE. A very rich silk often interwoven with gold thread.

SANGUINE. Scarlet.

SATIN FUGRE. Figured satin.

SARCIATUS or SARZIL. A coarse woollen cloth.

SAY. A woollen cloth, sometimes a silk textile.

SCAHWERE. A veil.

SCLAVYN. A pilgrim's overgarment like a long garnache.

SEINT or SEYNT. A Girdle.

SICLATON. Same as Baudekin, thirteenth century.

SIDE GOWN. Long Gown.

SINDON. A fine linen cloth.

SINGLE GOWN. An unlined gown.

SLOPPE. ? A jacket in the fourteenth century.
  Shoe or a cassock in the fifteenth century.
  Breeches in the sixteenth century.
  'Slops . . . have been "everything by turns" and certainly "nothing long" . . . , and the name is now most appropriately assigned to slop-sellers, who are dealers in all sorts of old clothes' (Planché, 1876).

SPANG. A metal fastening.

STAMEL. A coarse woollen cloth, generally red. Cf. Stamin.

STAMFORTIS. A strong and costly cloth (Anglo-Norman).

STAMIN. A worsted of a coarse kind.

SEQUANIE or SOSQUENIE.
SUKKENYE.
SUPERTOTUS.
} A loose frock worn over their other clothes by countrywomen (Chaucer)

TACHE. A clasp.

TARTARYN. A costly mediaeval stuff, the nature unknown.

TAVESTOCKE. A Broadcloth.

TAWNY. A dusky brown-orange colour.

TEMPLYS. Templettes (Frènch). 'My grete templys with the baleys (pale rubies).' Will of Countess of Warwick [1439].

TIPPET. Confusion arises from the word's having been applied to three different articles.

(1) A liripipe. 'With his typet ybound about his head' (Chaucer). 'thi typet as longe as a streamer that hangeth longe behinde and keepeth thee not hot' [1401].

(2) A cape. 'They be not all clerkes that have short typettes [1481].

(3) A pendant from the elbow of the cote-hardi (q.v.).

TOLEY. Scarlet.

VAIR. Fur of grise made up in squares from back and belly of the animal.

VERMEL. Vermilion.

VOLUPERE. A nightcap, fourteenth century.

WADMOL. A coarse cloth.

WATCHET. A sort of blue cloth.

WEDE. }
WEYD. } A garment.

Where "Halliwell" is mentioned above the book referred to is:
JAMES O. HALLIWELL (afterwards HALLIWELL-PHILLIPS) *A Dictionary of Archaic and Provincial Words* . . . 6th Edn. Routledge, 1847.

Bibliography

For convenience of reference the under-mentioned works are grouped according to their principal service for the student. Publication is in London unless otherwise stated.

1. *General, covering the Middle Ages in England with illustrated text.*

BOEHN, MAX VON. *Modes and Manners* [Middle Ages to Eighteenth century] translated by J. Joshua. (Vol. I.) Harrap, 1932.

BOUCHER, FRANCOIS. *A History of Costume in the West* (1965). Trans. J. Ross, Thames & Hudson, 1967.

FAIRHOLT, F. W. *Costume in England*. 4th Ed. (Edited H. A. Dillon). 2 Vols. Bell, 1909. Volume 2 is an illustrated glossary.

HARTLEY, DOROTHY. *Mediaeval Costume and Life* . . . Batsford, 1931. Elementary treatment. Notes on making costumes.

KELLY, F. M. and SCHWABE, R. *A Short History of Costume and Armour* . . . *1066–1800*. Batsford, 1931. The medieval section has a good text.

NEVINSON, JOHN L. 'Civil Costume' in Sir F. M. Powicke (ed.). *Mediaeval England*. Oxford Univ. Press Edn. 1950.

PLANCHE. J. R. *Cyclopaedia of Costume or Dictionary of Dress* (2 Vols.) Chatto and Windus, 1876-79. Fully illustrated.

SHAW, HENRY. *Dresses and Decorations of the Middle Ages* . . . (2 Vols.) Pickering, 1843.

STRUTT, JOSEPH (1) *A Complete View of the* . . *Dress and Habits of the People of England* . . . (2 Vols. folio). Edwards, 1796-9. Dates, sources and details of some · of the plates unreliable. Edited by J. R. Planché (Bohn, 1842) with some corrections; some of the plates coloured arbitrarily.

(2) *Manners and Customs of the English* . . . (3 Vols.) Published by author, 1775-6.

2. *General, covering the Middle Ages in France.*

ENLART, CAMILLE. *Le Costume* (*Manuel d'Archaeologie Française III*). Paris. Edns. 1916 and 1927. The careful analysis of details makes it invaluable for the English student where costumes of the two countries correspond.

EVANS, JOAN. *Dress in Mediaeval France*. Oxford, Clarendon Press, 1952.

LACROIX, PAUL. (1) *Manners, Customs and Dress during the Middle Ages and During the Renaissance Period*. Chapman and Hall, 1874. [Translated from the French].
(2) *The Arts in the Middle Ages*. 1875.

PITON, CAMILLE. *Le Costume Civil en France du XIII au XIX Siècle*. Paris, Flammarion. [No date].

3. Special Subjects.

CUNNINGTON, PHILLIS and BUCK, ANNE. *Children's Costume in England. 1300-1900*. Black, 1965.

CUNNINGTON, PHILLIS and LUCAS, CATHERINE. *Occupational Costume in England, Eleventh Century to 1914*. Black, 1967.

GODDARD, EUNICE, R. *Women's Costume in French texts of the Eleventh and twelfth Centuries*. Baltimore, Johns Hopkins Press, 1927. Contains a useful glossary of terms and textual quotations for a period insufficiently treated by most writers.

HARMAND, ADRIEN. *Jeanne d'Arc, ses Costumes, son Armure*. Paris, 1927. Dealing mainly with French costume of the fifteenth century; the author's exhaustive researches are nevertheless applicable in the main to England. A work which no serious student can afford to ignore.

LINTHICUM, M. C. *Costume in the Drama of Shakespeare and his Contemporaries*. Oxford, University Press, 1936.

LUNQUIST, EVA R. *La Mode et son Vocabulaire. Quelques termes de la mode feminine au moyen âge . . .* Goteborg, 1950. Gives contemporary quotations from French and English sources of women's costume details in the Middle Ages.

OAKESHOTT, WALTER. *The Artists of the Winchester Bible*. Faber and Faber, 1945.

OURSEL, CHARLES. *La Miniature du XII siècle à l'Abbeye de Cîteaux d'après les manuscrits de la Bibliothèque de Dijon*. Dijon, 1926.

WHITELOCK, DOROTHY. *Anglo-Saxon Wills.* Cambridge University Press, 1930.

4. *Books especially useful for their illustrations.*

EVANS, JOAN (ed.). *Flowering of the Middle Ages.* Thames and Hudson, 1966.

HARTLEY, DOROTHY and ELLIOT, MARGARET. *Life and Work of the People of England.* Vol. 1. *Middle Ages.* Batsford, 1931.

LONSDALE, H. W. and TARVER, E. J. *Illustrations of Medieval Costume.* Pubd. by the authors, 1874. Full of useful sketches from original sources. Slight text.

MILLAR, ERIC. *English Illuminated MSS.* Vol. 1. *X-XIII Centuries.* Paris, Lib. Nat. D'Art . . . 1926.

MITCHELL, SABRINA. *Mediaeval Manuscript Painting.* Weidenfeld and Nicolson (The Contact History of Art), 1964.

OAKESHOTT, WALTER. *The Sequence of English Medieval Art, illustrated chiefly from Illuminated MSS, 650-1450.* Faber and Faber, 1950.

RICKERT, MARGARET. *Painting in Britain—The Middle Ages.* (Pelican History of Art Series), 1954.

5. *Monumental and other Church Carvings.*

BOND, FRANCIS. *Wood-carving in English Churches. Vol.* 1. *Misericords,* Frowde, 1910.

CHANCELLOR, F. *The Ancient Sepulchral Monuments of Essex.* (Folio). Chancellor, 1890.

FRYER, ALFRED. *Wooden Monumental Effigies in England and Wales* Stock, 1924.

GARDNER, ARTHUR. (1) *English Medieval Sculpture* [new edition of his 'Handbook . . .'] Cambridge University Press, 1951 Excellent illustrations from photographs.

(2) *Alabaster Tombs of the Pre-Reformation Period in England.* Cambridge University Press, Edition of 1940.

[GOUGH, RICHARD.] *Sepulchral Monuments in Great Britain,* 5 parts, folio. Plates by Basire. Published by the author. 1786.

PRIOR, EDWARD, S. and GARDNER, ARTHUR. *An Account of Medieval Figure-Sculpture in England*. Cambridge University Press, 1912. Numerous photographs.

STONE, LAURENCE. *Sculpture in Britain in the Middle Ages*. (Pelican History of Art Series), 1955.

STOTHARD, C. A. *Monumental Effigies of Great Britain*. (Folio). New edition, 1876.

6. *Monumental Brasses.**

BOUTELL, CHARLES. (1) *The Monumental Brasses of England*. Bell, 1849. Numerous fine engravings, brief descriptions.

(2) *Monumental Brasses and Slabs . . . of the Middle Ages*. Bell, 1847. Includes drawings and descriptions of costume details.

COTMAN, JOHN SELL. *Engravings of Sepulchral Brasses in Norfolk and Suffolk*. (Folio). 2 Vols. 2nd edition, Bohn, 1839.

PAGE-PHILLIPS. *Children on Brasses*. Allen & Unwin, 1970. (Large paperback).

TRIVICK, HENRY. (1) *The Craft and Design of Monumental Brasses*. John Baker (now A. & C. Black), 1969. Profusely illustrated by "positive" facsimiles in gilt.

(2) *A Picture Book of Brasses in Gilt*. J. Baker, 1971. A smaller book, complementary to (1).

WALLER, JOHN G. and WALLER, LIONEL, A. B. *A series of Monumental Brasses from the thirteenth to the sixteenth Century* [drawn and engraved by the authors]. 1842-64.

7. *Illuminated MSS and Facsimiles.*

Specially rich sources are illuminated MSS in the British Museum, the Bodleian Library, Oxford, and the College collections in Oxford and Cambridge. A number of the most useful MSS have been well reproduced in whole or in part: notable are the following:

Queen Mary and *Luttrell Psalters*. [Fourteenth century] pubd. by B.M., respectively in 1912 and 1932.

*Brasses are instructive for costume details but occasionally the dates they bear mislead. Each portrays the fashions belonging to the date of its *construction* and this was sometimes years after, or even before, the date of the death commemorated.

Holkham Bible Picture Book. [*c.* 1330]. Dropmore Press, 1954.

Illustrations of the Book of Genesis. [*c.* 1360]. Oxford, Roxburghe Club, 1921.

Apocalypse in Latin. ['Dyson-Perrins MS. 10' (mid-thirteenth centry.)] Oxford University Press, 1927.

Pageant of the birth . . . of Richard Beauchamp, Earl of Warwick. [1485–90]. Ed. Viscount Dillon and W. H. St. J. Hope. Longmans, 1914.

Several great English MSS in the series 'Faber Library of Illuminated MSS' (in colour) Ed. by F. S. R. Boase, Faber and Faber.

Illustrations of a Hundred MSS. in The Library of H. Yates Thompson. Vol. 4. [English MSS twelfth to fifteenth centuries] Chiswick Press, 1914.

The Drawings of Matthew Paris. Walpole Society, XIV.

English Illumination of the thirteenth and fourteenth Centuries, a booklet pubd. by the Bodleian Library, 1954.

A Book of Old Testament illustrations of the thirteenth Century. [Pierpont Morgan MS M. 638]. Roxburghe Club, 1927.

See also *Millar, Eric* (above).

8. *Some Primary Sources quoted (Short titles).*

Edward II, Wardrobe Accounts. Archaeologia XXVI, 318-345.

Edward IV, Wardrobe Accounts. B.M. MS Harl. 4780.

Elizabeth Queen to Henry VII, Coronation, etc. B:M. MS Cot. Julius B XII. Published in John Leland's *Collectanea* IV (Edn. 1770).

Fastolf, Sir John's Inventory [1459] *Archaeologia* XXI, 252.

Henry, son of Edward I, Wardrobe . . . Hilda Johnstone, 1923.

Howard Household Books, see p. 168, Footnote.

Ordinances of Apparel [*c.* 1493] B.M. MS Harl. 1776.

Philippa, Princess: Trousseau [1406]. *Archaeologia.* LXVII, 217 seqq.

9. *Bibliographies.*

ANTHONY, P. and ARNOLD, J. *Costume—a General Bibliography.* Costume Society; Victoria & Albert Museum, 1968.

MONRO, I. S. and COOK, D. E. *Costume Index,* a Subject Index . . . New York, Wilson, 1937. Supplement, 1957.

Sources of Illustrations

Where the reference to a source book is incomplete full particulars will be found in the Bibliography.

Abbreviation B.M. — British Museum.

Frontispiece

    B.M. MS. Roy. 2A XXII, f. 219 (13th c. addition by School of Matthew Paris).

1. (a) and (d) 'Caedmon's' Metrical Paraphrase of Scripture History. Oxford Bodleian Library MS. Junius 11.
   (b) and (c) Benedictional of St. Aethelwold. B.M. MS. Add. 49598.
2. (a) and (b) Carolingian Bible. B.M. MS. Add. 10546.
   (c) Benedictional of St. Aethelwold. B.M. MS. Add. 49598.
3. (a) and (b) Ibid.
4. (a) B.M. MS. Cot. Tiberius C.VI, f.8.
   (b) B.M. MS. Cot. Tiberius B.V, Pt. 1, f. 34.
   (c) B.M. MS. Cot. Claudius B.IV, f. 66v.
   (d) Ibid. f. 43.
5. (a) Bayeux Tapestry.
   (b) (c) and (f) B.M. MS. Cot Claudius B.IV, ff. 54v, 55 and 36v.
   (d) and (e) B.M. MS. Cot. Tiberius C.VI, f. 13.
6. (a) (b) and (c) B.M. MS. Cot. Claudius B.IV, ff. 50v., 41 and 66v.
   (d) B.M. MS Harl. 2908, f. 64v.
   (e) B.M. MS. Cot. Cleo C.VIII, f. 8v.
7. (a) Winchester Bible. Winchester Cathedral Library. (Figure in initial to Isaiah with buckle added from initial to Micah.)
   (b) (d) and (e) St. Swithun's Psalter. B.M. MS. Cot. Nero C.IV, ff. 11 and 7v.
8. (a) (c) (d) and (f) Ibid ff. 25, 11, 11, 15.
   (b) Winchester Bible, Winchester Cathedral Library.
   (e) B.M. MS. Roy. 6 C.VI, f. 6.
   (g) Oxford. Bodleian Library, MS. Gough Liturg. 2, f. 17.
   (h) Effigy of Richard I at Fontévraud (detail). (From C. A. Stothard's 'Monumental Effigies of Great Britain').
9. (a) (b) (e) (f) and (g) Bury St. Edmund's Bible. Cambridge. Corpus Christi College, MS. 2, f. 94. [(e) and (g) composite].
   (c) Guthlac Roll. B.M. MS. Harl. Roll Y.6.
   (d) Bestiary. Oxford. Bodleian Library, MS. Ashmole 1511.

10. (a) Sculptured figure, Rochester Cathedral. W. Doorway. (Neckline reconstructed from Chartres Cathedral sculptures).

    (b) Winchester Bible. Winchester Cathedral Library.

    (c) York Psalter. Glasgow. Hunterian Museum, MS. U.3.2.

    (d) and (e) B.M. MS. Cot. Nero C.IV.

11. (a) and (b) Ibid.

    (c) and (d) Oxford. Bodleian Library, MS. Douce 293, ff. 9v. and 13.

    (e) Psalter of Westminster Abbey. B.M. MS. Roy. 2 A. XXII, f. 13v.

    (f) Oxford. Bodleian Library, MS. 269.

12. (a) Oscott Psalter. B.M. MS. Add. 50,000, f. 8.

    (b) Apocalypse. Formerly Dyson-Perrins Collec., MS. 10. (From facsimile, Montague James, O.U.P. 1927).

    (c) 'Bible Moralizée'. B.M. MS. Harl. 1527 (After f. 11).

    (d) Oxford. Bodleian Library, MS. 86 Arch.B. (From J. Strutt's 'Dress and Habits of the People of England').

13. (a) Chronicles by Matthew Paris. Cambridge. Corpus Christi College, MS. 26, f. 27.

    (b) and (c) Lives of Kings Offa I and II by Matthew Paris. B.M. MS. Cot. Nero D. 1.

    (d) Chronicles by Matthew Paris. Cambridge. Corpus Christi College, MS. 16, f. 70v.

    (e) Chronicles by Matthew Paris. B.M. MS. Roy. 14 C. VII.

14. (a) New York. Pierpont Morgan MS. M.638, f. 17v. (From facsimile in 'Book of Old Testament illustrations of the Middle of the 13th Century' by S. Cockerell and M. R. James, 1927.)

    (b) Chronicles by Matthew Paris. B.M. MS. Roy. 14 C. VII.

    (c) and (d) As for Fig. 12(b). (Apocalypse ff. 7v. and iv.)

    (e) Chronicles by Matthew Paris. Cambridge. Corpus Christi College, MS. 16, f. 95.

    (f) From Planchés 'Cyclopaedia of Costume', Vol. I. After a mural painting.

15. (a) Chronicles by Matthew Paris. Cambridge. Corpus Christi College, MS. 16, f. 182.

    (b) B.M. MS. Add. 38116 (Huth MS. iii), f. 11.

    (c) Chronicles by Matthew Paris. Cambridge. Corpus Christi College, MS. 26, f 11.

16.   Effigy, at Westminster Abbey, of Aveline, Countess of Lancaster. (From Stothard).

17. (a) and (b) B.M. MS. Sloane 3983, ff. 20v. and 30.

    (c) and (d) Venice. Bibl. Marciana, MS. 2397. (From S. Mitchell's 'Medieval Manuscript Painting', 1965).

18. (a) Oxford. Bodleian Library, MS. Rawl. A. 384.

    (b) As for Fig. 12(b). (Apocalypse, f. 35v.)

(c) Effigy, Scarcliff Church, Derbyshire. (From Stothard).

(d) Sculptured figure, Chartres Cathedral (N.Porch).

19. (a) and (d) Luttrell Psalter. B.M. MS. Add. 42,130.

    (b) B.M. MS. Add. 12228, f. 125v.

    (c) B.M. MS. Roy. 19 D. II.

20. (a) to (d) Luttrell Psalter B.M. MS. Add. 42,130.

21. (a) After a miniature in MS. 'Déduits de la Chasse' by Gaston 'Phoebus'. Paris. Bibl. Nat. (From Lacroix).

    (b) to (e) Luttrell Psalter. B.M. MS. Add. 42,130.

    (f) and (g) Queen Mary's Psalter. B.M. MS. Roy. 2 B. VII, f. 196v.

22. (a) (d) (e) and (f) Holkham Bible Picture Book. B.M. MS. Add. 47, 682, ff. 5, 7 and 12.

    (b) and (c) B.M. MS. Roy. 19 B. XV, ff. 24v., 23v. and 10.

    (g) Brass. St Margaret's Church, King's Lynn. (From Cotman).

23. (a) Psalter of Robert de Lisle. B.M. MS. Arundel 83.

    (b) Queen Mary's Psalter. B.M. MS. Roy. 2 B. VII.

    (c) Luttrell Psalter. B.M. MS. Add. 42,130.

24. (a) to (e) Ibid.

25. (a) to (h) Excluding (c). Ibid.

    (c) B.M. MS. 10292, f. 55.

26. (a) (b) (d) and (e) Luttrell Psalter. B.M. MS. Add. 42,130.

    (c) Misericord. Gloucester Cathedral.

    (f) B.M. MS. Roy. 6 E. VI, f. 9.

27. (a) to (e) Luttrell Psalter. B.M. MS. Add. 42,130.

28. (a) and (b) Queen Mary's Psalter. B.M. MS. Roy. 2 B. VII.

    (c) 'An English Mediaeval Sketchbook'. Cambridge. Magdalene College, Pepysian Library, MS. 1916.

29. (a) B.M. MS. Add. 47682. (b) Luttrell Psalter. B.M. MS. Add. 42,130.

    (c) (d) and (e) Queen Mary's Psalter. B.M. MS. Roy 2 B. VII.

30. (a) and (b) After B.M. MS. Roy. 15 D. II [From J. Strutt (1)].

    (c) and (d) Luttrell Psalter. B.M. MS. Add. 42,130.

31. (a) Brass. South Acre Church, Norfolk. (From Cotman).

    (b) Brass. St. Margaret's Church, King's Lynn. (From Cotman).

32. (a) Effigy of Wm. of Hatfield, 2nd son of Edward III. (d. 1344, aet. 8yrs.). York Minster.

    (b) Wooden effigy of Walter de Helyon, Much Marcle, Herefordshire.

33. (a) and (b) B.M. MS. Roy. 1 E IX, f. 230.

    (c) Weeper on tomb, Reepham Church, Norfolk. (From Stothard).

    (d) From Viollet-le-Duc's 'Dictionnaire . . . du Mobilier . . . ' III, 293, after a design on an ivory mirror frame.

34. (a) B.M. MS. Roy. 20 C.VII, f. 51.

    (b) Contemporary drawing of Black Prince, from a Royal Pedigree parchment roll.

(c) After a MS. Bible. The Hague. Mus. Meermano-Weestrianum. (From C. Enlart).

(d) After a MS. ex Royal Library, Paris. Bibl. Nat.

(e) and (f) Epistle of P. de Maizières to Richard II of England. B.M. MS. Roy. 20 B. VI, f. 2.

35. (a) Brass, once in St. Margaret's Church, Kings Lynn. (From Gough).

(b) 'Liber Regalis'. Westminster Abbey Library MS.

(c) Winchester Cathedral, window.

(d) to (h) Wall paintings in St. Stephen's Chapel, Westminster. (From Planché's 'Cyclopaedia of Costume' Vol: I).

36. (a) to (d) Diagrams based on Strutt (1).

(e) 'Liber Regalis', Westminster Abbey Library MS.

(f) (g) and (h) 'Chroniques de St. Denis' B.M. MS. Roy. 20 C.VII, ff. 75 and 47.

37. (a) Brass. Winterbourne Church, Glos. [From Boutell (1)].

(b) Brass, once in Ingham Church, Norfolk. (From Cotman).

(c) Monochrome of Jeanne de Bourbon. Detail from the Narbonne altar frontal. Paris, Louvre.

(d) From tomb of Edward III, Westminster Abbey.

38. (a) Effigy. St. Mary's Church, Warwick. (From Gough).

(b) Sculpture of Jeanne de Boulogne Duchesse de Berry. Poitiers, Palais de Justice.

39. (a) Brass. Wood Ditton Church, Camb. [From Boutell (1)].

(b) Brass. Spilsby Church, Lincs. [From Boutell (1)].

(c) Effigy. East Harling Church, Norfolk. [From Gardner (2)].

40. (a) Effigy. Canterbury Cathedral. (From Stothard).

(b) Misericord. Gloucester Cathedral. (From a photograph by S. Whiteley).

41. (a) Brass. Ore Church, Sussex. [From Boutell (1)].

(b) Brass. Northleach Church, Glos. [From Boutell (1)].

(c) Brass. Kinston-upon-Thames Church, Surrey. [From Boutell (1)].

42. (a) 'Les Très Riches Heures du Duc de Berry.' Chantilly, Musée Condé.

(b) and (c) 'Le Champion des Dames' by Martin le Franc. Brussells, MS. 9466, f. 1.

(d) Life of St. Edmund. Translation by John Lydgate. B.M. MS. Harl. 2278, f. 37.

43. (a) Detail from a drawing in 'Planet Venus,' a Franco-Burgundian MS. Dresden. (Colours based on contemporary illuminations).

(b) John Foxton's 'Cosmographia'. Cambridge, Trinity College.

(c) Thomas Occleve's 'De Regimine Principum.' B.M. MS. Arundel 38.

44. (a) Weeper on tomb at Elford Church, Staffs.

(b) and (c) Detail of a tapestry at Hardwicke Hall, Derbyshire. [Reproduced in colour in Connoisseur III (1902)].

(d) and (e) Lydgate's Life of St. Edmund. B.M. MS. Harl 2278, f. 55v.

45. (a) Jean Fouquet. The Martyrdom of St. Apollonia (detail).
  (b) 'Hours of Etienne Chevalier,' Jean Fouquet. Chantilly, Musée Condé.
  (c) From a photograph of a tapestry in the Burrell Collection, Glasgow.
  (d) Detail from a Missal, reproduced in A. Harmand's 'Jeanne D'Arc.'
  (e) From Harmand (re-drawn).
      N.B. (a) (b) (c) and (d), although taken from sources belonging to
      the 2nd half of the 15th c., are equally illustrative of the 1st half.
46. (a) Brussels, MS. 10958.
  (b) From a photograph of a tapestry in the Burrell Collection, Glasgow.
  (c) Brass. St. Stephen's Church, Norwich. (From Cotman).
  (d) Diagrams of the pattens in (e). (From Harmand).
  (e) J. van Eyck. Portrait of J. Arnolfini and his wife (detail). London,
      National Gallery.
  (f) From Planchés's 'Cyclopaedia of Costume' Vol. I.
47. (a) Lydgate's 'Sege of Troye.' Manchester, The John Rylands Library.
  (b) and (e) 'Les Très Riches Heures du Duc de Berry.' Chantilly, Musée
      Condé.
  (c) (f) and (g) B.M. MS. Roy. 20 C.VII.
  (d) Lydgate's Life of St. Edmund. B.M. MS. Harl. 2278, f. 19.
48. (a) to (d) 'Hours of Elizabeth the Queen.' B.M. MS. Add. 50,001.
  (e) Lydgate's Life of St. Edmund. B.M. MS. Harl. 2278, f. 19.
  (f) J. van Eyck. Portrait of Bauldwyn de Lannoc. Berlin.
49. (a) Brass. St. Giles' Church, Norwich. (From Cotman).
  (b) Effigy. Lingfield Church, Surrey.
  (c) Painted panel illustrating The Life of St. Etheldreda (detail). London,
      Society of Antiquaries.
  (d) 'Hours of Elizabeth the Queen.' B.M. MS. Add. 50,001.
  (e) A Hatter's Seal. (From Harmand).
50. (a) and (b) Effigy. Ashwelthorpe Church, Norfolk. (From Stothard).
  (c) B.M. MS. Cot. Julius E. IV art. 6, f. 5.
51. (a) Brass, Tilbrook Church, Bedfordshire. [From Boutell (1)].
  (b) Brass, Sawtry Church, Huntingdonshire [From Boutell (1)].
  (c) Brass. Castle Donington Church, Leicestershire. [From Boutell (1)].
52. (a) Brass. Spilsby Church, Lincolnshire. [From Boutell (1)].
  (b) After B.M. MS. Harl, 4431. [From Strutt (1)].
  (c) Brass. Bedington Church, Surrey. [From Boutell (1)]. Brasses'.
  (d) and (e) B.M. MS. Harl. 4431, f. 3.
53.   Brass of Joyce, Lady Tiptoft. Enfield Church, Middlesex. [Boutell(1)]
54. (a) Brass. Ormesby Church. Norfolk. (From Cotman).
  (b) B.M. MS. Harl. 2278, f. 115.
  (c) Misericord. Wellingborough Church, Northants. (after a photograph
      by S. Whiteley).
55. (a) Brass. Felbrigg Church, Norfolk. (From Cotman).

(b) Effigy. Over Peover Church, Cheshire.

(c) Effigy. Lingfield Church, Surrey.

56. Jan Van Eyck. Portrait of his wife. Bruges.

57. Effigy. Ashwelthorpe Church, Norfolk. (From Stothard).

58. (a) Effigy. Hoveringham Church, Notts. (From Stothard).

(b) Effigy. Wingfield Church, Suffolk. (From Stothard).

59. (a) Effigy of Jeanne de Montejean at Bueil, Indre-et-Loire, France.

(b) Petrus Christus. Nativity. (Detail).

(c) Effigy. Arundel Church, Sussex. (After a photograph in A. Gardner's 'Alabaster Tombs').

60. (a) Jean Fouquet and successor. The Building of the Roman Wall. Paris, Bibl. Nat. MS. fr. 20071-2.

(b) and (c) Wall paintings. Eton College Chapel, Windsor.

(d) '. . . Life . . . of Richard Beauchamp, Earl of Warwick, (1389-1439)' B.M. MS. Cot. Julius E. IV art. 6, f. 5v.

61. (a) Master of King René. 'Cuer d'Amours Epris'. Vienna. Nationalbibl. Cod. 2597.

(b) Jean de Vavrin. Chronicles of England. Vol: i, B.M. MS. Roy. 15 E.IV, f. 14.

62. (a) Portrait of Philippe le Bon — detail of an illumination in Jean Miélot in Brochart's 'Advis Directifs.' (From Piton).

(b) Detail from 'The Vision of St. Bernardino' (French School). Marseilles, Musée Grobet-Labadié.

(c) B.M. MS. Cot. Nero D. IX, f. 49.

63. (a) Jean Fouquet. 'Le Jugement de Duc D'Alencon'. Munich, Staatsbibl.

(b) Jean de Vavrin. Chronicles of England, Vol 3. B.M. MS. Roy. 14. E. IV.

(c) Miniature from 'Livre des Comptes' of the Brotherhood of Charité-Dieu.

64. (a) B.M. MS. Cot. Julius E. IV, art. 6, f. 5.

(b) 'Trial of Weights and Measures . . . ', B.M., a Harl. MS. reproduced in Vetusta Monumenta Vol. I. (1746).

65. Jean Fouquet. Portrait of Etienne Chevalier (detail). Berlin.

66. (a) Dirk Bouts. 'La Justice d'Othon' (detail).

(b) Master of King René. 'Cuer d'Amours Epris'. Vienna, Nationalbibl. Cod. 2597.

(c) '. . . Life of . . . Earl of Warwick.' B.M. MS. Cot. Julius E. IV. art. 6, f. 5v.

(d) After a painting in the Musée d'Arts Décoratifs, Paris. (From C. Piton).

67. (a) Detail from miniature of 'Philippe le Bon et son Secrétaire' in the Chronicle of Hainault. Brussels, Bibl. Roy. MS. 9244.

(b) and (d) Gerard David. Judgment of Cambyses (detail). Bruges.

(c) From Planché's 'Cyclopaedia of Costume' Vol. 1. (after a French painting).

68. (a) Ibid. [Diagrams to explain fig. 68 (b)].

(b) B.M. MS. Cot. Julius E. IV art. 1, f. 5.

69. (*a*) Portrait of Edward IV. London, Society of Antiquaries.
    (*b*) Dirk Bouts. Portrait of a Man. London, National Gallery.
70. (*a*) (*d*) and (*e*) B.M. MS. Cot. Julius E. IV art. 6, ff. 10, 11 and 14.
    (*b*) 'Roman de la Rose.' B.M. MS. Harl. 4425, f. 184v.
    (*c*) Effigy. Norbury Church, Derbyshire.
71. (*a*) Wall painting. Paris, Palais du Trocadéro.
    (*b*) Brass. West Harling Church, Norfolk. (From Cotman).
    (*c*) Wall painting. Eton College Chapel, Windsor.
72. (*a*) (*b*) and (*c*) B.M. MS. Cot. Julius E. IV art. 6, f. 22v.
    (*d*) Wall painting. Eton College Chapel, Windsor.
73. (*a*) French tapestry.
    (*b*) B.M. MS. Roy. 16 F. II, f. 188.
74. (*a*) Oxford. Bodleian Library, MS. Douce 213.
    (*b*) Wall painting. Eton College Chapel, Windsor.
    (*c*) B.M. MS. Roy. 15 E.VI, f. 403.
    (*d*) Effigy. Brancepeth Church, Durham. (From Stothard).
75. Petrus Christus. Portrait of a Young Woman. West Berlin.
76. (*a*) Petrus Christus. Legend of St. Eloi (detail). New York, Metropolitan Museum.
    (*b*) Brass. Sherbourn Church, Norfolk. (From Cotman).
    (*c*) Brass. Iselham Church, Camb. (From Gough).
77. (*a*) Roger van der Weyden, Portrait of a Lady. Mellon Collection.
    (*b*) Portrait of Guillemette de Vergy. (Burgundian School). Worcester, U.S.A., Art Museum.
78. (*a*) and (*b*) '. . . Life . . . of Richard Beauchamp, Earl of Warwick, 1389-1439' B.M. MS. Cot. Julius E. IV art. 6, f. 23v.
    (*c*) B.M. MS. Roy. 16 F. II, f. 188.
    (*d*) Brass. Merton Church, Norfolk. (From Cotman).
79. Maître de Moulins. Portrait of Duchess Anne de Bourbon (detail). Moulins Cathedral.
80. (*a*) B.M. MS. Cot. Tiberius B.V, f. 8v.
    (*b*) B.M. MS. Cot. Nero C. IV, f. 42v.
    (*c*) B.M. MS. Harl. 2278, f. 68v.
    (*d*) Holkham Bible Picture Book. B.M. MS. Add. 47, 682.
    (*e*) Cambridge. Fitzwilliam Museum, MS. 370.
    (*f*) B.M. MS. Egerton 1894, f. 26.
    (*g*) and (*h*) B.M. MS. Harl. 2278.

Index

(*See* Glossary for terms not defined in the text and for list of materials and colours not directly referred to in the text. Additional sources and references are contained in the Bibliography. Glossary, pages 182 to 189. Bibliography, pages 190 to 194. For sources of illustrations, *see* pages 195 to 201).
Italicised figures are page references to illustrations or Plate references to the three illustrations in colour.